*Praise for Bruce Junes's Jokes*

"*Some of these stories caused me to laugh so hard, I had tears in my eyes and my assistant thought I was having an apoplectic fit.*"

-- A senior executive who asked to remain anonymous to save himself from embarrassment.

"*There's one story in here that is so funny, I almost had an accident in my underwear.*"

- - A company president whose identity must be withheld to preserve his dignity.

"*I would like to complain about that 'I, Robot' story. It caused me to pull a muscle in my cheek from laughing so hard.*"

-- Published letter to the Editor of the <u>Globe & Mail</u>. They settled out of court.

"*I've been reading Bruce's stories for years. Now, just opening the paper to his column brings on the giggles.*"

--A well-respected professor who admits she's also extremely ticklish.

"*Well done! Well done!*"

-- Waitress shouting Bruce's hamburger order to the cook.

*To Neil & Virginia*

*Keep Smiling!*

# Humour on Wry, with Mustard

## 88 Tasty Treats to Feed Your Funny-bone

### Bruce Gravel

*Bruce Gravel*

### Illustrations by Bob Sherwood

**Wigglesworth & Quinn**
Peterborough

HUMOUR ON WRY, WITH MUSTARD

Published by: Wigglesworth & Quinn, Peterborough, Ontario, Canada
Ordering Information: bruce@brucegravel.ca
Printed in the United States of America

First Edition: May 2008


**Library and Archives Canada Cataloguing in Publication**


Gravel, Bruce M. (Bruce Magnus), 1952 -
    Humour on wry, with mustard: 88 tasty treats to feed your funny-bone / Bruce Gravel; illustrations by Bob Sherwood. -- 1st ed.

Includes Index.
ISBN 978-1-4382-0056-9

    1. Canadian wit and humour (English). I. Title.

PS8613.R369G73 2008        C818'.602        C2008-902020-0

*Everything is better with mustard.*

This book is dedicated with love
and the greatest appreciation to
Frances and Scott,
the most loyal cheering section that
anyone could hope for.

# Acknowledgements

The hilarious illustrations in this book were done by Bob Sherwood, a professional caricaturist living in Ontario. Contact Bob at: 905-659-5498. Email: cartoonbob@cogeco.ca.

Many thanks to Frances Gravel for her great work in the formatting and lay-out of the entire book, getting it all print-ready, including the back cover.

Many thanks also to Scott Gravel, for designing the front cover and electronically enabling the printing of this book.

Most of the stories in this book previously appeared in the Peterborough Examiner newspaper from June 2003 to March 2008, and are reproduced here with their permission. Special appreciation to Columns Page Editor Rob McCormick.

The story "I, Robot, Defy You" previously appeared in the Globe and Mail newspaper, August 13, 2004.

My hugest thanks go to Frances and Scott for their wonderful inspiration, honest feedback, and unfailing encouragement to my tales and this project.

*Bruce Gravel*
*Peterborough, Ontario*
*March 2008*

# Menu

## Chapter One: Family

To My Brother, Who Tempts Fate     *14~*
*(Tinkering can be an electrifying experience)*

Creatures of the Night     *16~*
*(Differing approaches to a bat in our belfry)*

Wet Behind the Ears     *19~*
*(When disaster strikes, go shopping)*

Symphonie Nocturne     *21~*
*(My family's Music of the Night)*

Our Son, the TV Psychic     *23~*
*(Uncanny predictions)*

Murder, She Planned     *25~*
*(Family plot has grave implications)*

SWM Seeks SWF.  Object: Acrobatics     *27~*
*(Technosavvy twentysomethings try to get dates)*

Getting Her Just Desserts     *29~*
*(Eating dessert first threatens the natural order)*

Caught Between Fire and Ice     *31~*
*(A bride vs. her mother-in-law, with me in the middle)*

Living with The Change     *33~*
*(Winds blow hot, winds blow cold, male sailors take warning)*

Pimp My Husband     *35~*
*(An automotive make-over of a rusty old consort)*

The Street That Disappeared     *37~*
*(Be careful what you wish for)*

Going Squirrelly     *39~*
*(My mom's war at home)*

## Chapter Two: Friends & Neighbours

A Tale of Two Blinkys     *43~*
*(Dog-eared next-door neighbours)*

The Wandering Dock     *45~*
*(A gypsy jetty refuses to settle down)*

Little Mosque on the Water     *47~*
*(A boatload of new Muslim in-laws)*

Not a Teddy Bears' Picnic     *49~*
*(Dumb luck saved their lives)*

Where, Oh Where Did Our YCRY Go?     *51~*
*(The Circle of Life in neighbourhoods)*

Feline Follies     *53~*
*(Which are smarter: cats or dogs?)*

20,000 Leagues under Katchawanooka     *55~*
*(Strange sights mystify the locals)*

## Chapter Three: Living

"Hello, I'm from the Government"     *58~*
*(The phone survey from hell)*

Out of the Hamper     *60~*
*(It's true! Men can do the family laundry)*

Beware Trojan Horses     *63~*
*(Inventions that promised to make our life easier)*

Two Words That Guarantee a Happy Marriage     *65~*
*(Be very careful how you say them)*

This Is a Job for Cyber Sleuth     *67~*
*(Be wary of what you overhear)*

Just Do It!     *69~*
*(Long-time couples don't need to ask permission)*

Snow and Tell     *71~*
*(The dog days of spring)*

Oh, for the Sounds of Silence     *73~*
*(Seasonal insanity, every fall)*

So Many Choices, So Little Time     *76~*
*(The perils of sending a male to buy groceries)*

No Sex Please, I'm Toxic     *78~*
*(A tale of two raccoons with intimacy problems)*

Hold the Phone!     *80~*
*(That evil invention torments us still)*

What Your Teen Needs Most　82~
*(An essential item for parents with teenagers)*
What Chicken Tastes like　84~
*(An age-old mystery solved)*
Sales by Symbology　86~
*(Raptors and panthers and bears, oh my!)*

## Chapter Four: On the Job

I, Robot, Defy You　89~
*(Artificial Intelligence proves how dumb it can be)*
The Sea Wolf　92~
*(The night an adult timber wolf went downtown)*
My Time as a Woman　94~
*(Water and Kleenex don't mix)*
Why Restauranteurs Get Grey　96~
*(That's not a kilt!)*
Meetings Etiquette Sorely Lacking　98~
*(Drastic remedies for bozos who disrupt meetings)*
The CEX Show　101~
*(Clear communication vital to continued survival)*
Peterborough after Dark　103~
*(People change when the sun goes down)*
Trafficking　105~
*(Life in the slow lane)*

## Chapter Five: Holidays & Special Occasions

The True Meaning of Christmas (Carols)　108~
*(What olde tyme lyrics mean today)*
More True Meanings of Christmas (Carols)　110~
*(Modern interpretations of other olde lyrics)*
How the Government Stole Christmas　112~
*(Bureaucratic Grinches take over)*
O Christmas Tree　115~
*(A snow-bound family outing)*

*R*eindeer Calling Cards     *117~*
*(The perils of over-decorating)*
*C*racking the Christmas Code     *119~*
*(What merchandise and retailer messages really mean)*
*N*ew Year's Unresolutions     *121~*
*(Undaunted, unimproved, unrepentant - so there!)*
*L*ove Is a Many-splendored Thing     *123~*
*(We're going to need a bigger card shop)*
*C*upid Go Home     *125~*
*(If Cupid were around today, he'd be smothered in lawsuits)*
*P*ut-upon Pops     *127~*
*(The burdens placed upon fathers)*
*F*ather Knows Last     *129~*
*(Why do kids always go to mom first?)*
*W*hy Are Fathers So Special Anyway?     *131~*
*(Why dads deserve their day)*
*M*otel Macabre     *133~*
*(Hallowe'en hospitality at its best)*
*I*t's Not Easy Being Green     *135~*
*(Choose your Hallowe'en costume wisely)*
*C*elebrating Birthdays     *137~*
*(Casinos outdo relatives with many happy returns)*

## Chapter Six: Pleasures & Pastimes

*G*etting into Hot Water     *140~*
*(The naked truth about spa etiquette)*
*D*aring the Wind     *142~*
*(A sailor gets upset)*
*I* Was a Garage Sale Gremlin     *144~*
*(Some people should never host garage sales)*
*a*dventures in Sushi     *146~*
*(The joys of eating raw fish off almost-nude females)*
*T*oday's Wonder Women     *148~*
*(Female handypersons take over)*
*C*aught in a Mid-life "Car-sis"     *150~*
*(Seduced by exotic models)*

*M*id-life "Car-sis": the Sequel     *152~*
*(Sir, you're drooling on the chrome)*

*A*re We There Yet?     *154~*
*(Road trip checklist: luggage, maps, kids, tranquilizers)*

*W*hat Am I Bid for this Husband?     *156~*
*(Why I'm banned from attending auctions)*

*C*hocolate Caribbean Conundrum     *158~*
*(Practical jokes on the high seas)*

*H*ave Shorts, Will Travel     *160~*
*(Cultural differences bedevil travellers)*

*H*owdy, Davy-san     *162~*
*(A trilogy of tall travel tales)*

*C*offee, Tea, or Naked Frauleins?     *164~*
*(Fringe benefits while travelling)*

*D*ances with Dolphins     *166~*
*(It must be my animal magnetism)*

*O*f Pirates and Parrotheads     *168~*
*(Buffetted about in Margaritaville)*

*C*lose Encounters on the Trail     *170~*
*(Ever see a tree growing out of a cyclist's back?)*

*M*y Summer Concussion     *172~*
*(Getting attention - the hard knocks way)*

*L*uring Lady Luck     *174~*
*(How gamblers try to influence slot machines)*

*F*ly like an Eagle     *176~*
*(Land like a dodo)*

*T*he Eagle Has Plotzed     *178~*
*(What goes up, comes down badly)*

## Chapter Seven: Off the Wall

*W*hat If Superheroes Really Existed?     *181~*
*(Spidey, it's about the goo...)*

*R*etired Superhero Reunion     *183~*
*(Time has not been kind to these caped crusaders)*

*T*he Caped Stocking Stuffer     *185~*
*(Comic books have really changed since we were kids)*

Graveyards of Bad Ideas                                   *187~*
    *(Where flops rest in peace)*
How to Slow down Time                                     *190~*
    *(How bald men can become useful to society again)*
The Domestic Olympics                                     *192~*
    *(Sports events around the house)*
Wacky in Wackimac                                         *194~*
    *(Nutty naysayers numb a small city)*
Bath Butler, Personal Therapist, or Thong?               *196~*
    *(Hotel amenities we'd like to see)*
Party Favours                                             *199~*
    *(Political parties we'd sure enjoy)*
Factory Seconds We'd Rather Not See                      *202~*
    *(Even if the price is right)*
The Wise Man's Wife                                       *204~*
    *(Answers to 15 of life's Big Questions)*

## An Extra Helping of Dessert

An excerpt from                                          *206~*
    Bruce Gravel's upcoming new humour novel,
    **Inn-Sanity: Diary of an Innkeeper Virgin**

# Chapter One

## Family

# TO MY BROTHER, WHO TEMPTS FATE

*Tinkering can be an electrifying experience*

They say certain things run in families, like hair loss, politics, "big bones" and buck teeth. In my family, where nobody runs, a wonderful mechanical aptitude occurs, passed down from father to son. Unfortunately, in my case, this aptitude leap-frogged over me and landed on the second child, my brother.

My dear old dad was a born tinkerer. He could fix or assemble just about any mechanical thing without referring to an owner's manual. What he fixed actually worked too, which distinguished him from many of those who believe owner's manuals are a senseless waste of trees.

Yet he had certain work habits that contradicted his normally careful practices. For one thing, he kept me around to help when he fixed engines, despite my difficulty learning which end of a torque wrench was which. This tended to slow his projects down somewhat.

As another example, whenever dad worked on his car, he had a lit cigarette hanging from his mouth. Often, the engine would be running with him bent over it, tuning it up - cigarette glowing brightly. Didn't seem that safe to me, so I always kept my distance. Probably another reason why I didn't learn much about motors.

My brother proudly carries on in dad's footsteps. He scoffs at owner's manuals and loves tinkering with engines. Thankfully, he doesn't have dad's habit of smoking around gasoline, but he has developed other - unique - work habits.

Like when he's deep inside his car engine, adding a new chrome-plated high-performance framistat, and he needs to strip a wire. Instead of wasting precious time searching for a wire stripper or pair of pliers, he uses the natural equipment God gave him: his teeth.

Sometimes, he discovers the wire is live - the hard way. Yet the resulting electric shock is always mild, which reassures him that using pliers is as unnecessary as owner's manuals.

Having used his chompers for years in this manner, he thought nothing of stripping other wires the same way.

Until that fateful day last winter when he was remodeling his teenage daughter's bedroom, installing boyfriend-proof bars on the windows, motion-sensors on the door, and other doting-dad type stuff.

When he was relocating her land-line phone, he needed to strip the phone wire to reconnect it. Of course, the pliers were in their detached garage, a distance that seemed like miles away in the 40-below Edmonton weather.

Drawing on the vast storehouse of logic accumulated over decades of cheating death or serous injury while tinkering, he reasoned that if the shock was mild when he stripped thick car wires with his teeth, then it should be minuscule with the thin phone wire.

So he bit the wire with his teeth.

The shock burned his moustache, blackened his lower face, and caused a yelp so loud his son heard it over the blaring TV. My brother found himself sitting down, dizzy and smoking.

Clearing his head with a few swigs from the beer bottle that was an essential part of his toolbox (occupying the space where a wire stripper or pliers should be), he decided the shock had been an anomaly. Besides, the phone wire still needed stripping and the garage was still miles away.

So he bit it again.

He really appreciated the flowers I sent him while recuperating in hospital.

Duct-taped to the vase was a brand-new wire stripper.

*(I never strip wires with my teeth. That's what my wife's potato peeler is for.)*

# CREATURES OF THE NIGHT

*Differing approaches to a bat in our belfry*

According to sacred comic book lore, Bruce Wayne was sitting in his study late one night, brooding over what costumed persona he should adopt to strike fear into criminals (widely known as a superstitious and cowardly lot), when a giant bat crashed through the window.

"Aha!" said Bruce. And so The Batman was born.

When a bat entered our house recently, the reaction was somewhat different.

"AAAH!" said Bruce.

"Calm down," said my wife. "It's only a little bat. And it won't fly into either of us, silly, so stop cringing. Especially you; your chrome dome is a perfect reflector for its sonar."

Nonetheless, as the expected defender of our household, I dove for the closet and emerged holding a bat of my own. The other kind, used by petulant millionaire ball players. I approached the winged rodent, gripping my weapon, ready for battle. Bat against bat.

"Keep calm! Don't get hysterical!" I yelled to my Better Half in an authoritative tone that somewhat concealed my own hysteria. "I'll soon put paid to this creature!"

I deftly manoeuvred around couch and coffee table, filled with savage triumph as I bore down on the beast, before gracefully sprawling headlong over an ottoman.

"No!" yelled She Who Commands. ""Don't hurt the poor thing! It just flew in here by mistake. There's an easier way to get rid of it."

It was obvious that blind panic had clouded her reasoning. Thank God I could still think clearly.

I jumped to my feet. Eons of primal hunter/killer instinct

coursed through me. The small black fiend zipped around our livingroom almost too fast for the eye to follow, taunting me. I felt myself giving in to the hard-wired male stress response: hit something.

As I stood there, a pot-bellied Babe Ruth waiting for the opportunity to belt Killer Bat out of the ballpark, my encyclopaedic brain swiftly reviewed what I knew of bat lore. The Little Brown Bat, *myotis lucifugus,* loved eating insects, especially mosquitos (so perhaps we should keep it around to help protect us from West Nile Virus?). However, it was also a fact, verified by countless movies, that many bats had the distressing habit of transforming into bloodsucking vampires. Was this one of those? Surely not; it seemed much too small. Perhaps it was rabid? Yes, that had to be it. Why else had it invaded our home, except in the throes of a crazed dementia similar to men doing all their Christmas shopping late on December 24? Any second now, it would alight on one of us, sinking its sharp fangs into our overtaxed Canadian flesh, then becoming furious upon realizing we had already been bled dry by our elected vampires.

I raised my weapon, my eyes tracking the intruder like a dog watching the approach of a full supper dish.

"You're mine, bat," I muttered. "Just slow down a bit and you're one dead varmint."

"Will you PLEASE put down that baseball bat, before you start swinging and break some of our stuff!" ordered the umpire. I growled in frustration, but complied. Thirty years of marriage had taught me that you don't mess with the ump.

"Good. Now I'll go open the back door, while you close all the doors leading into the livingroom except the one closest to the back door."

Ah! I understood her plan perfectly. Trap this creature of the night and smother it with a large throw pillow! Would cause far less damage than the baseball bat.

So I shut the required doors, grabbed a pillow from the couch, and slowly advanced towards the noxious beast. It had perched atop a bookcase and was trembling (an obvious ruse to elicit sympathy).

"Stop that!" barked you-know-who, re-entering the livingroom.

"We're not out to kill it, but to free it. Now, just walk towards it with your arms wide, get it flying again, but don't get between it and the one open door. We want it to find its way out of this room, and then go outside."

"Free it?" I said incredulously. "But it's vermin that invaded our home! We have the right to clobber it! It's in the Charter of Rights and Freedoms!"

She gave me The Glare. I did as instructed, still certain that only drastic measures, involving chasing and swearing, with a dash of blood-letting, would rid us of this nocturnal devil. Well, let us try it her way, then when that failed, she'll let me whack the beast a good one. I was positive I could accomplish the execution with only a minimum of property damage; a lamp or a plant at most. Maybe.

The creature became airborne again, circled the room once, then, like a bat out of you-know-where, darted through both the open livingroom door and the back door and was gone.

"There, see?" said She, with a smug look. "No muss, no fuss, no violence."

"Yeah.  Wonderful."  The hunter/killer urge reluctantly subsided, grumbling. "So, uh, how'd you know that would work?"

"Elementary, my dear goof: I know how their sonar works and figured the bat wanted out as badly as we wanted it out."

"Really? Huh."

So, besides her full-time paid job as Executive Assistant and her full-time unpaid duties as wife, mother, best friend, chef, shrink, nurse, painter, gardener, sanitary engineer, barber, judge, jury and executioner, my Better Half can now add another title to her lengthy resume: Master of Bats.

Batwife.


*(Hmmm, I wonder if she sneaks out at night dressed in a skintight black costume with a bat symbol on her chest and a flowing cape?  And if she does, do you think she'd let me be Robin?)*

# WET BEHIND THE EARS

*When disaster strikes, go shopping*

Years ago, when our son was only three, we took him to Los Angeles in March. While I spent my days trapped in a conference for association managers, my wife and son went on tours arranged by the conference organizers.

One such was a boat tour of the stars' waterfront homes. It was only after the tour bus collected my family, that they discovered said boat trip comprised only 25% of the excursion (and came last on the itinerary). The other 75% was visiting a floral nursery and a shopping mall. Major disappointment. Deposited at the mega-mall, my dynamic duo grudgingly explored it. Finally, with 15 minutes left before the tour bus departed, they plopped down on the rim of a wide fountain to rest. Spotting a fruit vendor, my wife turned to ask our son if he'd like a treat.

He was gone.

Milliseconds later, she heard a splash right behind her. Snapping her head around, she saw the water close over our son. The slippery little weasel had fallen in.

Hauling him out of the shallow water, she realized in horror that they were miles from our hotel, with no change of clothes, and a bus departing in 15 minutes for the boat dock.

Now had that been me, I would have begged a big garbage bag from a custodian, placed our dripping heir in it with his little blond head poking out, then cabbed it back to the hotel. Game over.

Not my wife. She paid for that tour and they both really wanted to go on the boat trip. But she didn't want our soaked sardine catching cold on the boat, either.

Sprinting into a nearby washroom, she shucked off his wet togs and dried him under the hand drier. Wrapping him in her sweater, she quickly located a children's clothing store, ran inside, and grabbed clothes in his size. As boys' underwear was only sold in packs of six, she seized a pair of girls' undies, hoping it wouldn't affect him later in life.

She dashed to the cash, giving the surprised cashier the clothes in the order needed to dress a child. The cashier scanned, then cut off, the tag on each item, while my wife dressed our son on the spot.

Asking directions to the nearest children's shoe store, she sprinted off, glancing at her watch.

Five minutes left.

She tore inside the shoe store, grabbed a pair of son-sized sneakers, and sped to the cash.

Three people were ahead of her.

She blurted out her need to pay for the shoes immediately, explaining that time and tour waited for no woman. The cashier archly stated that my wife would wait her turn. The people in line glowered, faces expressing disbelief in her story.

Muttering a phrase that would turn a California tan white, my wife left the shoes and bolted for another washroom. She put his sopping sneakers under the hand drier for several minutes, then snatched some paper towels and made it to the tour bus just as the doors were closing.

En route to the boat dock, she packed the sneakers with paper towels, drying them as best she could.

That evening, when I returned to our hotel room, our son proudly showed off his new set of clothes.

I failed to deduce what that meant. After whining about how I'd been cooped up inside at seminars all day, I remarked about how they must have enjoyed their relaxing boat tour.

At this point, my wife abandoned all the qualities of resolve and grace under pressure that she had demonstrated earlier in the day.

It would have been less painful if I had simply walked into a hornets' nest.

She should have been one of the experts on my conference's panel that afternoon: it dealt with Crisis Management.

*(I still walk into hornets' nests on occasion.)*

# SYMPHONIE NOCTURNE

## *My family's Music of the Night*

I write this at great personal risk, as you will understand when you read further.

Once the family that it shelters retires for the night, a house grows quiet. But not silent. Creaks and groans occur regularly, especially in winter after thermostats are lowered and timbers cool as outside cold invades. In some houses, other nocturnal noises occasionally intrude, like the plaintive cry of a child needing consoling from a nightmare, or the muffled weeping of NHL hockey fans at the latest loss of their favorite team.

At our house, the Symphonie Nocturne usually involves mysterious and sometimes frightening sounds reminiscent of large industrial factories, auto-crushing machines, and powerful turbo-prop aircraft engines coughing into reluctant life.

In other words: snoring.

Every single member of my household stoutly - and sometimes angrily - denies that they snore. Yet, as the nighthawk who is usually the last to climb into bed and then tries to get to sleep, I can attest that they do.

Sometimes it's quiet, almost peaceful, droning, like that of a large animal, say a lion or antelope, exhausted after a long day of chasing and being chased. Other times, the lion and antelope are stampeding madly across the plains, fleeing for their lives, chased by a herd of enraged bull elephants with yapping hyenas as outriders.

At times, the Nocturnal Symphony is abruptly interrupted, as if, mid-way through the concert, the orchestra suddenly refuses to play until their salary demands are met. Or you wonder if they have just suffered a group heart attack. The silence is deafening, an almost physical assault on your eardrums. Worried, you hold your breath. Then, just as suddenly and with a rasping groan like your Grandpa's ancient Chevy struggling to life in 30-below weather, the performance resumes, louder than before. Your breathing also resumes.

Also amazing is how coordinated the concert is. Normal orchestras play together in one place, but my family's symphony is performed by chainsaws in separate rooms. Yet the performance is beautifully coordinated: one saw revs up while the other slows down, waiting for another log.

Measures to stop the snorer rarely work. Shoveling the slumbering body into a new position elicits grunts, protests, sometimes a physical counterattack - then, for all your trouble, stentorian breathing like that of a great whale resumes several minutes later. A pillow placed over the snorer's face is risky; there are laws about smothering someone to death. Unfortunately.

Some evenings, the volume is so loud that I wonder why the snorers don't jerk awake, startled. That's certainly what happens to me, sleeping amongst these busy factory workers.

Other nights, reading quietly in our livingroom, sudden sounds similar to rupturing pipes or a tree crashing through our roof, cause me to dash upstairs in a panic, only to find that it's the usual suspects serenading the world. Yowling cats in heat are quieter.

I'm embarrassed to admit that I am not musically inclined whatsoever. In our talented Von Trapp Family of musicians, I'm the guy selling tickets out front. Hotly denying this, my son once surreptitiously captured me on video, snoring away like an asthmatic dragon. Well, it was faked; he dubbed the sound of a snorting hippo onto the tape. He has the technical skills to do this: he majored in TV Broadcast Production in college.

I sleep silent as a fawn. Ask anyone in my family.

***(Unauthorized copies of my son's video are available.)***

# OUR SON, THE TV PSYCHIC

## *Uncanny predictions*

Our son graduated college with a diploma in Television Broadcasting and, unlike his dad and many others, was fortunate enough to quickly land a job in his chosen profession. He works for a major national TV network in Toronto, in Master Control, which fortunately has nothing to do with taking over the world, and everything to do with making sure the right TV program gets aired at the right time with - and this is crucial - the right commercials.

Besides paying him to watch television eight hours a day, working at the network also unleashed our son's latent psychic abilities.

My wife and I first became aware of his hitherto-unknown psychic powers during the time contestant Ken Jennings was earning his way to super-stardom on *Jeopardy.* As each show started, our son predicted Jennings would win. He was always 100% correct. He even predicted the exact episode when Jennings' unprecedented winning streak would end. Right again.

He then started predicting major events on other shows we watched, like who was next to die on *Lost*, who would next jump into bed with whom on *Desperate Housewives*, and who committed the week's grisly murder on *CSI.* All as each show's opening credits rolled.

100% accurate, every time. (His reliable divinations only applied to television; he had the same luck we all have picking winning lottery numbers: abysmal.)

Amazed, my wife started humming the old *Twilight Zone* theme whenever our son made his perceptive prognostications. Equally amazed, I started thinking of ways to cash in on his newfound uncanny ability, like betting on the outcomes of televised sports events. In fact, why limit it to sports? Imagine predicting the outcome of a national election, before the TV networks did. Or who'd win the million on *Survivor.*

My tiny mind boggled.

Then I started to notice a pattern.

He refused to predict the outcomes of shows or sports events on networks other than his employer. He also never predicted the outcome of a live sports event, no matter what network aired it.

Hmmm.

Then one day, under threat of severe inhumane torture (no second helping of Mom's Awesome Lasagna), he finally revealed his secret.

Turns out the little weasel is no more psychic than the $2.95-a-minute hotline hucksters advertising on TV in the wee hours of the morning.

By virtue of his job, he has access to tapes of shows days in advance of their broadcast dates. Whenever he worked the midnight shift (his preferred shift, since pesky bosses are home snug in their beds), he watched these shows when his real work was done.

Then he'd astonish his gullible parents with his so-called psychic powers.

The brat.

(Brattiness comes from his mother's side of the family; everyone's a complete angel on my side. Four out of ten police officers will verify this.)

Now that his secret's out, he still tells us the outcomes of shows, totally ruining the suspense we get from watching them. Told you he was a brat. No longer Our Son The TV Psychic; he is now Mr. Spoil Sport.

In some countries, I hear it's a capital offense to ruin the ending of a TV show, movie, or novel. People get sent to prison for that. Or shot. Maybe we should do this in Canada, too. I"ll write my MP today - just as soon as I make a wager with a colleague on who will win *The Amazing Race.*

I got some inside information.

***(I also know who shot JR.)***

# MURDER, SHE PLANNED

### *Family plot has grave implications*

A female colleague where our son works in Toronto, said she read somewhere that all married women, at some point in their relationship, get fed up enough to concoct a plan to kill their husbands. She herself, after seven years of marriage, planned to do her hubby in with a wood chipper, just like in the movie *Fargo*. Having watched many episodes of *CSI* on TV, she outlined the careful steps she'd take to avoid forensic detection after her dastardly deed.

Our son unfortunately related this tale to my wife, whose eyes lit up at once.

"She has a plan to off her husband after only a measly seven years of marriage?" she said. "She's still a newlywed! Boy, have I ever been missing out - I've been married for 32 excruciating years! I've got a lot of catching up to do!"

I could tell her brain was already churning with possible ways to hasten my inevitable departure from this mortal coil. Our son grabbed some paper, eager to take notes.

I started to feel uneasy.

"It has to be unusual, unexpected," she mused. "Nothing mundane."

"So your cooking is out," I said. She shot me a withering look.

"How about the spa?" offered our son, always anxious to help his mother. "We could fill it with pirana and disconnect the underwater light. Then when Dad uses it at night, he won't see them."

"Yes, and when the water starts frothing around him, he'll think it was the spa jets making bubbles!" said my wife, rubbing her hands, obviously excited by the idea. "We'd only be left with bones to bury, and I know the perfect place to hide the evidence."

"Your garden!" I blurted, then wondered if perhaps I shouldn't be so helpful, considering the topic of conversation.

"Here's another idea," said our son, rapidly on his way to being cut out of my Will. "Dad likes sleeping in his hammock in summertime, right? So we get one or two big 30-foot pythons, put them up the trees his hammock hangs from, then let nature take its course when he lies beneath. The snakes will even dispose of the evidence for us, one gulp at a time."

"Great idea." I said sarcastically. They took it as encouragement and pressed on.

"Scaring him might bring on The Big One," said my wife. "Men his age are prone to heart attacks. He gets easily startled when he's working away in his noisy laundry room or workshop, his back to the door, and you come up behind him and say something loudly. The coroner would see it as sudden death by heart failure. We'd be completely in the clear."

"Gee, I had no idea you two would be so inventive at brainstorming my murder," I said, wishing I had a tape recorder running, to gather evidence. "Perhaps I should get a gun, for self-defense."

"Yeah, that's it!" said our son. "Then we could arrange a Hemingway - a fatal accident when you're cleaning it."

I glared at him, thinking that fatal accidents can work both ways, and said:

"Well, you two just better watch yourselves: I'm writing a story about all this, and when it's published, everyone will read about your evil plans, so you wouldn't dare off me after that."

They snorted in unison.

"Oh, c'mon Dad," said our son. "Don't you know that no one reads your stuff? Mom and I are safe as houses."

*(If you email me and I don't reply, please notify the police. They should check the garden first.)*

# SWM SEEKS SWF.
# OBJECT: ACROBATICS

*Technosavvy twentysomethings try to get dates*

It amazes me that many members of today's twentysomething and thirtysomething generations still face the same challenge that we of the dinosaur generation had when we were their age:

Getting a date.

Once a person has finished their schooling and plunged into the hurly-burly working world, some find it hard to make a date connection. This is astounding, considering all the electronic means now available: Facebook, Youtube, MySpace, text-messaging, blogging, personal websites ("sexydevil.orgy"), I-Phones, Palm Pilots, Palm Co-Pilots, Global Positioning Satellites, neural implants, and so on.

In my day, millennia ago, before Steve Jobs had taken a bite of his first Apple, when we were casting for post-graduate dates, we relied on social groups, church gatherings, clubs, dances, parties at friends' houses, chance encounters at grocery stores, arranged encounters at auntie's house, and so on.

In short, face-to-face, instead of Facebook.

Nowadays, groups and clubs meet via online "chat rooms", church services are on television, groceries are ordered over the Internet, and auntie is off touring the world with her fourth husband.

In today's e-age, there's precious little face-to-face interaction. Younger folks have no idea how to go about it. Take away their electronic gizmos, and they're as helpless as a bureaucrat tasked with streamlining paperwork.

For instance, take my e-savvy totally-plugged-in twentysomething son (please). He's a college graduate, holds two well-paying jobs, has money in the bank, owns a late-model car, and is very well-travelled. He is bright, articulate, funny, and can talk your ear off on the issues of the day. Despite his father's genes, he's good-looking with a full head of hair.

You'd think women would be lining up to go out with him (did I mention he can also cook?).

Yet he has great difficulty in getting a date.

Maybe it's because he has those two jobs, meaning he usually works seven days a week. Perhaps it's because he often works the midnight-to-eight shift and sleeps during the day; it's hard to socialize with that schedule, unless you're courting Dracula's daughter.

Or it could be that he's related to me.

But all that shouldn't matter, what with the plethora of electronic aids available to connect with potential dates.

However, it seems the potential dates are themselves too busy pursuing careers to invest in a little in-person socializing. Either that, or they're wary of someone who keeps a vampire's hours.

His current dilemma is that he purchased two prime-seat tickets for the August 16 performance of the new Cirque du Soleil show, *Kooza*, in Toronto. So far, he's been unable to secure an occupant for the seat next to his. Everyone he's asked is either too busy, has a time conflict, or wouldn't know what the world-famous Cirque du Soleil is if the troupe's Grand Chapiteau (Big Top) fell on them.

He's becoming convinced the dating pool has been drained, right in the middle of the summer swimming season.

I'd like to help him out.

So, dear readers, if any of you are, or know someone who is, a twentysomething non-smoking single female with an interest in the outstanding acrobatics and hilarious clowning of Cirque, preceded by a delightful dinner, and wouldn't mind a date with a really nice person, then please contact me.

Otherwise, he'll be forced to take his dad to the show, and sit there totally embarrassed when that dad jumps up on stage and joins the Cirque clowns mid-way through their performance. (It's happened before.)

*(My non-profit dating service is now open.)*

# GETTING HER JUST DESSERTS

*Eating dessert first threatens the natural order*

WARNING: do not let your children read this story!

My wife causes quite a stir whenever we eat in a restaurant. Not because she loudly proclaims herself as a well-known food critic, so her meal better be good. (It's me that always says that.) It's because she smiles sweetly at the wait staff - and orders dessert first. And she wants it brought when the rest of us get our main course.

The reaction of the wait staff is usually priceless: it ranges from disbelief to amusement to disapproval and, sometimes, that look people get when confronted with someone who's obviously a bit addled.

Once, a diner at the next table gaped at her and said: "You can't do that!"

"Yes I can," she replied. "My mom's not here."

See? It doesn't bother her in the least.

However, I'm quite concerned. There is a natural order to things, and we risk tampering with cosmic forces beyond our comprehension if we disrupt it.

Like broken resolutions follow New Years, like sleepless nights follow new babies, like rain follows getting your car washed, and like weddings follow pregnancies, certain things naturally occur in succession. The most important natural order of things is that desserts always follow the main course. It's been that way since cavepeople ate their first mammoth and finished off with a delicious chocolate torte. My wife strongly disagrees.

Years ago, while touring lovely P.E.I., we chanced upon a quaint out-of-the-way restaurant owned by beloved Maritimes singer Catherine McKinnon (married to Don "Charlie Farquharson" Harron). The first thing you see as you enter Catherine's eatery is a big display of awesome mouth-watering desserts. The second thing you see is this sign:

"Life is too short. Eat dessert first."

For my wife, that was the highlight of our trip. It vindicated her life-long practice of doing just that - whenever she could get away with it.

She is infamous at certain Peterborough restaurants as the lady who always flips to the back of the menu first. Later, while her dining companions chow down on their entree, she ecstatically devours some fluffy sugary confection. She explains that she is usually too full after the main course to have dessert, even if she forgoes the appetizer. And since desserts are usually the most exciting things on the menu, why not start with the best?

Besides, hard-working pastry chefs spend hours creating their exquisite decadent offerings. Imagine how they feel when folks fill up on the appetizer and entree, and have no room for dessert? There's weeping in restaurant kitchens across the land. (Which often dilutes the whipped cream.)

It's her self-proclaimed duty to stop those tears.

My wife has courageously shucked off the tyrannical rule of our well-meaning mothers: "finish your plate, or you won't get any dessert."

In other words, to paraphrase a Broom Hilda cartoon: "eat until you're stuffed too full, then as a reward, you'll get even more food." She thinks that particular logic makes about as much sense as the male compulsion, when watching their favorite sports team on TV, to enthusiastically cheer them on, because without that encouragement, their team would surely lose.

Now waitaminute: if she's able to disrupt the natural order by eating dessert first - and the world hasn't ended - then my son and I should have the same right to do some disrupting of our own. Specifically: eliminating something that "must" be part of every meal.

Vegetables. (Except for potatoes. Preferably French fried, garlic mashed, or scalloped.)

*(I contemplate world disorder, while rarely getting my just desserts.)*

# CAUGHT BETWEEN FIRE & ICE

*A bride vs. her mother-in-law, with me in the middle*

In the 1970s, two years after we were married, I returned to McGill University to complete my degree. Though my wife continued working to help support us, the only way we made ends meet was by moving into a low-rent basement apartment at my parents' Montreal house.

While it was "going home" for me, the experience was difficult for my bride. She not only had to put up with my peccadilloes, but those of my landlord parents as well, living above us.

The worse trial was my mother's cooking.

Now don't get me wrong: my French-Canadian mom was a great cook. We still use some of her recipes today.

However, she had a problem serving hot food. Her definition of "hot" was "lukewarm". To my wife, raised by a French-Canadian mother who served hot food at a temperature just this side of volcanic, my mom's food was always cold.

With a palate used to lukewarm food for 22 years, I had to make quite an adjustment after our marriage to the torrid fare my wife served. Many times she faked me out: setting steaming plates in front of us (I had no idea what waves of steam meant), she started eating with gusto and, human food vacuum that I am, I quickly followed suit.

And always got third degree burns in my mouth.

She never gave me any sympathy, saying I could always wait and let it cool down. She didn't understand that, where I grew up, you had to scarf down your warmish food immediately before it either got stone cold, or a sibling swiped it off your plate.

It was survival, man.

To stretch our meagre food budget, my parents periodically

invited us up from the cellar to have dinner with them. In the interests of detente, my wife gamely promised not to complain about the temperature of the food.

And she never did, bless her - until The Day of the Lasagna.

My mom made a wonderful lasagna. This particular day, however, her fondness for serving tepid grub hit a new low on the thermometer.

The pre-assembled lasagna went directly from freezer to oven, then after baking, to the table. When our plates were placed in front of us, I started devouring lasagna with reckless abandon (a bad habit since, as my wife oft reminds me, I could gobble down tainted food before realizing its "best before" date was in 1945).

Suspicious because no heat waves emanated from her meal, my wife gingerly took a small bite.

Cold.

She then cut into the centre of the pasta.

Her fork failed to penetrate.

In horror, she realized the centre was still frozen.

She shot me a desperate look, which turned to astonishment at seeing me wolf down a dinner that concealed an iceberg.

Despite what she had promised, she couldn't bring herself to eat a lasagna-cicle. She spoke to the chef, which caused great consternation, apologies, and further heating until the ice at least melted.

My dad wisely ignored all this and concentrated on the TV news.

During the three years we lived beneath my parents, I was caught between two extremes of fire and ice: basement food served by a wife whose definition of "hot" would forge steel at a Hamilton foundry, and upstairs food from a mother whose definition of "hot" would suit a polar bear during the Arctic winter.

Novelist Tom Wolfe was right: you can't go home again.

*(I should be thankful I get fed at all. However, I still burn my mouth.)*

# LIVING WITH THE CHANGE

*Winds blow hot, winds blow cold, male sailors take warning*

When women reach a certain age, they embark upon the grand adventure known as the Change of Life.

That means their Significant Others get shanghaied upon the same adventure. Even if you're not packed for the trip, you're going, buddy. It's quite an epic journey: full of hills and valleys, swamps and summits. Perils lurk around every corner. Travelling companions sometimes wonder if they'll live to see another day. Nightly prayers for divine protection become commonplace.

The term "mood swings" is cruelly deceiving. It implies a pleasurable playground activity. The correct term should be: Rollercoaster From Hell.

To the uninitiated, a Change of Life might mean a new job, new home, new lifestyle, (or sometimes a new spouse). But the true Change is like all of the above - all at the same time. Worse, it includes volcanic hot flashes. Arctic cold spells. Restless nights of only three or four hours sleep.

All of which affects everyone in the immediate vicinity, Significant Others most of all. It's more nerve-wracking than hosting a birthday party for an entire Grade One class.

There are dozens of books and hundreds of articles available to counsel women on this tumultuous mid-life journey. There are support groups, medical advice, and medication both natural and manufactured.

But there is precious little for the Significant Others. We're left to fend for ourselves in a hostile environment, with no map, a broken compass, rapidly-diminishing supplies, alligators snapping at our heels, and a Force Five hurricane bearing down on us.

For guys, it's more traumatic than a power failure in the middle of the Super Bowl.

Those accompanying their captains on their lengthy voyage of Change can relate to Captain Bligh's crew, who cast him adrift in a longboat, then sailed off to idyllic Pitcairn Island in the South Pacific. Some days, escaping to your own tropical island is very tempting. But you didn't hear that from me.

Medical science is still debating whether or not male menopause exists. Women fervently hope it does; revenge is sweet.

I used to admire those intrepid men who, in ages past, embarked upon long sailing voyages of exploration. Perilous and life-threatening trips that meant years away from home.

I now realize why they did it. They figured they had better odds of survival than if they stayed home with wives undertaking their own years-long, arduous voyage. Cannibals and typhoons were nothing, in comparison. (At least those explorers could sleep snugly, instead of having their blankets torn off whenever their partner had a nighttime hot flash.)

However, those adventurers weren't really all that brave. In fact, they were total cowards. Disappearing when their lifemates needed them most.

Men owe it to their ladies to be there during this difficult time, considering everything women put up with from us, including our sports obsessions, like the all-important hockey, baseball, football, basketball, golf, soccer, lacrosse, NASCAR, ping-pong and tiddledywinks seasons.

Some female readers may be thinking: "what do *you* have to complain about, dead meat? *We're* the ones who have to endure this terrible ordeal!"

That's very true. I certainly don't mean to belittle women's suffering. I was merely pointing out that most women don't go through it alone. So perhaps, if it please the court, a small modicum of the slightest bit of sympathy might possibly be extended to the Significant Others.

Or at least give us a handbook. It's the humane thing to do. ("What's that, dear? Do what with my handbook?")
Never mind.

*(I'm living life on the edge.)*

# PIMP MY HUSBAND

*An automotive make-over of a rusty old consort*

Our son convinced my wife and me to watch one of his favorite TV shows: *Pimp My Ride*. To our relief, it has nothing to do with prostitution, and everything to do with a complete make-over of someone's vehicle  Each episode, a rusty, beat-up, outdated car, truck or van, is completely transformed into a thing of beauty.

At the conclusion of the show, my wife opined that it's too bad the show's automotive make-over experts didn't offer the same service for husbands.

Uh-oh. Was that some kind of sly disparaging remark?

Was I really a candidate for a make-over?

While I wasn't looking, have I morphed from sleek sports car to dowdy sedan? After over three decades of dependable use to my original owner, did she see me as rusty and outdated, with sagging chassis, leaky transmission, and a dragging trunk?

As objectively as possible, I took stock of myself.

**Chassis:** still quite sound, despite the mileage.  In fact, it's a 1950s classic (or is that now an antique?).  Bones solid and in good working order; no broken parts.  Muscles functioning, though in desperate need of a tune-up.

**Body:** defined as what covers the chassis, some serious bodywork is required here.  No rust, but lots of superfluous material which needs to be trimmed off, to enhance performance and reduce weight on the springs.  Sandpaper alone won't suffice; this job calls for heavy-duty grinders. New paint job wouldn't hurt either.

**Trim:** original factory equipment generally still in place (teeth, nose, ears, etc.), except for head hair: roof has been transformed from a soft-top to a hard-top. Direct sunlight or bright lights cause blinding glare, resulting in serious road hazard for oncoming traffic.

**Upholstery:** seat is definitely better padded than when model was new. However, what I consider an asset, others consider a liability. Don't know why.

**Headlights:** bulbs certainly not as bright as before, resulting in impaired vision. However, corrective lenses enable driver to spot a skimpy bikini at 100 yards, just like in younger days.

**Engine:** heart still ticks over reliably, though takes longer to reach top speed than in earlier years. Now works better on premium fuel, than when younger, when any old fuel would do. Sometimes wonder if engine will start on very cold mornings.

**Fuel consumption:** definitely higher than when first manufactured. Richer mix in later years results in far fewer kilometers to the litre.

**Electronics:** on-board computer brain still fairly sharp. However, occasional programming lapses are irritating. Certain electronic commands to the rest of the machine sometimes take much longer to activate required mechanical response (eg: repairing stuff, yard work, or taking out the garbage).

**Fluids:** all hoses and clamps still at full integrity; no leakages yet.

**Handling:** depends on who's driving, especially around tight curves.

**Exhaust:** nothing wrong there. Definitely far more active than in earlier years. Lemon-scented catalytic converter needed to spare the immediate environment.

Reviewing my self-diagnostic, my wife admitted that it was fairly accurate. However, she said a trained mechanic would be better qualified to give a proper assessment. (If the needed repairs were too expensive, would she trade me in for a newer model?)

I was disappointed with her suggestion of a mechanic; I thought I had sufficient diagnostic expertise.

In fact, I was preparing to do a similar evaluation on her.

Perhaps it's best if I don't; that might get me sent straight to the auto recyclers.

*(I have the mind of a Ferrari in the body of a Lada. Honk if you understand.)*

# THE STREET THAT DISAPPEARED

*Be careful what you wish for*

This is a true story. Let's say it happened in the capital of the province that's Canada's economic engine: PEI.

For years, my aunt and uncle have lived on a quiet street. (Let's call it Anaconda Court.) Right across from the entrance to their street, on the other side of a connecting boulevard, was Anaconda Crescent. (The bureaucrat in charge of street names had been tired that day.)

Watering the seeds of a future identity crisis, the bureaucrat gave the houses on both streets the exact same numbers.

This caused untold hilarity over the years.

Once, an entire truck load of topsoil was dumped at Number 7 Anaconda Court, when it should have been delivered to Number 7 Anaconda Crescent. While the homeowner on Court was pleased with the unexpected bounty, his counterpart on Crescent was a tad upset, especially when the bill arrived.

One day, my aunt answered her doorbell and was astonished to see the workings of a brand new gas furnace strewn upon her front lawn, chaperoned by an impatient installer. Told she never ordered a new furnace, indeed she was quite happy with her present one (there wasn't even a gas line going to her house), the installer coloured the air a lovely shade of blue until he double-checked his work order and saw Crescent in the address, not Court.

Countless pizzas and Chinese dinners were delivered to homes that never ordered them. Gorgeous flowers for anniversaries and birthdays likewise got misdelivered. (Once the unintended female recipients took possession, just try retrieving them. Reloading a huge load of topsoil was far less hassle.) Entertainment for stag parties arrived at the wrong houses (and was rarely refused).

But there was a darker side to these confused identities.

Ambulances screeched to a halt at the right house number, wrong street. And were half-way back to base before they noticed a relative of the injured chasing them, screaming "STOP!".

Police and fire calls were likewise misplaced, shocking occupants of the innocent homes, while giving burglars and flames precious extra minutes to do their mischief.

So my uncle spearheaded a neighbourhood petition to have Anaconda Court renamed something completely different: Burmese Python Court.

Food, flower and furniture deliveries depended on it. Lives too. It was a no-brainer. He lobbied the city bureaucracy for five years and got nowhere.

Finally, a sympathetic civil servant took pity and altered my uncle's application to imply a major new housing development, generating major new tax revenue, necessitated the name change. The change was approved within a week.

But there was an unforseen side effect: their street disappeared. No city map or directory showed a Burmese Python Court.

Mail wasn't delivered. No mail meant no bills. This was no cause for celebration. No bills meant no property taxes, or water, phone, hydro and cable bills, could be paid - causing houses to be threatened with seizure and endangering essential services. Their street never got plowed after blizzards, because it simply didn't exist on the plow crew's map. Police, fire and ambulance couldn't respond. Pizzas and Chinese food went cold in delivery cars. (Oddly enough, Jehovah's Witnesses continued to ring their chimes with no trouble at all.)

After a stressful year of trying to get their new name noticed, the final insult came last Hallowe'en: Their shiny new Burmese Python Court street sign was stolen. They have now effectively ceased to exist. Their children and grandchildren are traumatized.

Now they understand the old Chinese proverb: "Be careful what you wish for, because you may get it."

*(It's odd, but I don't remember having relatives in Charlottetown.)*

# GOING SQUIRRELLY

*My mom's war at home*

My mother hated squirrels with a passion equaled only by the furry critters' love of her corn.

During my teenage years (150 years ago), she planted several rows of corn each spring in her vegetable garden behind our suburban Montreal home, then over the next three months, tried to keep the developing cobs safe from marauding squirrels. It was always a tight race as to who would enjoy the fruits of her labours first: us or the varmints.

The varmints usually won.

Though grossly outnumbered, my mom was not one to admit defeat. As with all wars, her squirrel conflict escalated over the years.

At first, she shooed them away from the corn whenever she saw them: charging out of the house hollering and waving a broom, bearing down on the mooching rodents like an avenging Valkyrie.

Great entertainment for the neighbours.

I think the squirrels were amused too.

When that proved both ineffective and exhausting, she set humane cages to trap them, then drove great distances to release her captured prisoners. (She never calculated the gas expense of this catch-and-release effort, compared to the cost of simply buying corn at the Farmer's Market. My dad did, but wisely held his tongue.)

For two years, she chauffeured kidnaped squirrels by the bushel, only to have four-legged reinforcements move in to continue the war.

So she changed tactics and placed a brown paper bag over each ear of corn, reasoning that "out of sight, out of mind."

She discovered the thieving beasts had a great sense of smell.

She then declared Total War.

My dad, a consummate handyman, was conscripted to build a gigantic chicken wire cage around the entire corn patch, including a wire roof. This massive fortress had a large door, so mom could tend her crop. Convinced that squirrels possessed the same cunning dexterity of raccoons, who could undo latches (perhaps the raccoons held seminars for the squirrels?), she padlocked the door.

The Cage didn't work. Squirrels are either great diggers, or great lock-pickers.

Next spring, she had my father sink chicken wire three feet down in the earth all around the cage. When Stalag Gravel was completed, I solemnly proclaimed that no corn cob would ever escape.

She was not amused.

Inside the Stalag, she again covered the ears with paper bags. Extra security.

Ears still got eaten.

Now at her wit's end, she took drastic measures. It was wartime, after all.

I came home from school one afternoon, and was immediately hit with the distinctive smell of gunpowder as I stepped into the house. My adolescent brain slowly realized that -

*KA-CHOW!*

A thunderous roar came from my brother's bedroom.

Distressed that my brother had committed suicide before he repaid the money he owed me, I dashed into the bedroom, which overlooked the backyard vegetable patch.

I saw my mother lower her smoking rifle from the open window, a grim smile on her face.

"That's one damn squirrel who will never eat my corn," she muttered, as she ejected the spent shell.

The bright brass casing clanged on the polished hardwood floor; a scene from some Hollywood crime flick in which I had suddenly become a bit player.

Trained in her teens to be a hunter by her dad, she obviously still had her skills years later.

I babbled that firing a gun in suburbia was probably illegal.

She retorted that was why she fired from inside the house, stupid boy, so the neighbours wouldn't notice.

She spotted another bushy-tailed bandit and smoothly swung the rifle onto her shoulder. Hawkeye Jenny took careful aim, gently squeezed the trigger, the gun boomed, and I fled the room.

My dad eventually brokered a cease-fire between her and the rodents.

To ensure a lasting peace, he hid her bullets.

*(I do not own a gun or grow corn, so squirrels frolic in complete safety at my house. Now cats, on the other hand...)*

# Chapter Two

## Friends & Neighbours

# A TALE OF TWO BLINKYS

## *Dog-eared next-door neighbours*

When coincidence, an essential and overused ingredient of many movie and mystery novel plots, happens in real life, it can be hilarious. Case in point:

Our neighbour inherited her mother's dog, after mom passed away. Let's call her "Blinky" (the dog, not the neighbour. I've changed the name to protect the embarrassed.)

Blinky is a small poodle with an large attitude problem. (She is also expensive; since being bequeathed, she has racked up over $4,000 in vet's bills.)

About a year after Blinky acquired her new servants, a new neighbour moved in next door. By coincidence, the man of the house had an unusual nick-name:

Blinky.

(You can see where this is going.)

Barely unpacked, sitting on his verandah sipping his morning coffee, the new neighbour was startled to hear an exasperated female voice bellow:

"Blinky! Get over here! Right now, you naughty so-and-so!"

Spewing out a mouthful of perfectly-good java, the newly-arrived Blinky asked his wife:

"Is that lady next door calling to me? And how does she know my nick-name; we haven't even met yet!"

His wife regarded him with a classic "and what have YOU been up to, Mister?" look.

"Blinky! Come here, you little Dickens! And stop licking yourself!"

Both jaws of the new neighbours fell open. The man stood and looked over the high fence. He saw a lady in the next yard, standing with her hands on her hips, addressing something near the ground.

"I, um, think she's talking to a shrub," murmured the two-legged Blinky. The lady then demanded he accompany her for "walkies". He whispered to his wife: "Let's go inside. Quietly."

A few days later, Blinky the Biped was soaking in his outdoor spa, when this imperious command thundered from the other side of the fence:

"Blinky! Get out of that water this instant! Company's coming and I don't want you dripping all over the house!"

Shocked, the man rose and peeked over the fence. He saw the lady wagging her finger at a flower-filled urn next to her pool.

Blinky settled back to his soak, only to hear the lady threaten to haul him down to the clinic for a distemper shot.

That weekend, Blinky was severely reprimanded for digging in the neighbour's flower garden. He assured his astonished wife that he had never gone near that flower bed, much less dug in it. His wife wondered if they'd have to move again.

Then he asked if he needed a haircut, because that lady had said he looked like a shaggy dog.

The last straw came the next day, as the Blinky family were enjoying a picnic lunch on their deck. Somewhere between the fried chicken and dessert, came this loud entreaty from next door:

"Come here, Blinky! I've got a yummy treat for you! You'll really like it!"

"I don't care if she is maybe a little touched," said Blinky's wife. "You march over there and tell her to stop bothering you."

"Yeah," said Blinky. "But first I wanna see what kinda treat she has for me."

Then the lady promised an extra-special treat after today's visit to the doctor - to get fixed! That did it.

Blinky stomped up to the fence, ready to do some bellowing of his own. He peered over and discovered there were two Blinkys, one with two legs and the other with four. And the poodle's embarrassed owner realized her commands were affecting two Blinkys.

However, months later, both Blinkys still look up expectantly whenever yummy treats are announced.

*(I will do tricks for yummy treats.)*

**44~**

# THE WANDERING DOCK

*A gypsy jetty refuses to settle down*

Friends of ours bought a house on the western shore of Chemong Lake, north of Peterborough, Ontario, the first time they owned waterfront property.

A watercraft was obviously called-for, so they boldly purchased a sleek two-person pedal boat, complete with jaunty canopy.

Such a mighty vessel demanded a suitable dock. So our friends commissioned an expert in such matters - their landscaper - to construct one forthwith.

Used to constructing sturdy retaining walls, the landscaper built quite the wharf: a massive rectangular wooden behemoth that was capable of berthing the *Titanic*. It was so heavy that a crane was needed to hoist it off the lawn into the water.

Both dock and pedal boat were thoroughly enjoyed by our friends last summer, their first on the lake.

Then the fall arrived; that depressing time when boats, golf clubs, sports cars, halter tops and docks are put away for the winter. Not this dock, though. It was far too heavy to be hauled out.

However, their nautical landscaper had a solution: the beast would be cast off from shore and anchored in deeper water for the winter. The theory was that when the lake froze over, the dock would be far enough away from the grinding shore ice to be safe.

By December, that theory had yet to be tested, as we had unseasonably mild temperatures. But our friends had other problems. Seems that, once released from bondage to the land, that dock developed a passion for travelling; a wanderlust equaled only by politicians on foreign "fact-finding" missions.

Being on the windward side of Chemong, their property is frequently smacked by high winds and waves. Ideal conditions for a wandering wharf.

At first, the thing took short trips, testing its newfound freedom. It visited first one, then the other, neighbour's beach, on either side of our friends' property. Towed back and re-anchored each time, it tugged at its tether sullenly, plotting its next Great Escape.

The day before Christmas, it really outdid itself. Our friends awoke, looked out, and saw that their jetty had eloped again.

After searching with binoculars, they located it: clear across the lake, almost at the opposite shore! That dock was so determined to roam, it had travelled *against* the prevailing winds.

How were they to recapture their errant floating lumber, when everyone's boat had been put away for the winter and all the marinas were closed?

Ever helpful, I suggested canoeing over and building a large billboard on it, turning it into a floating advertising platform, then letting it ramble up and down the Trent Severin Waterway as it wished. The sign could proclaim Peterborough's hallowed status as Lacrosseville, or promote our scintillating nightlife.

Another friend sagely observed that patience was needed, for if it really loved them, then it would return on its own.

Ignoring such excellent advice, our friends drove across the causeway to the leeward shore. Near where their vagabond quay bobbed offshore, insolent and unapologetic, they encountered two local gentlemen relaxing on their front porch, quaffing Christmas cordials and planning a huge New Year's Eve bonfire.

They were eyeing the wooden dock.

The men promised to tow the itinerant wharf back to its owners, come spring. Meanwhile, they tied it to a sturdy tree, to halt its walkabout. (Floatabout?)

Still, there are many months until spring, and who knows what will happen when the ice breaks up? Wanderlust is a powerful urge. So if you notice a gypsy jetty this spring, nuzzling against your own dock, perhaps with the romantic notion of making baby docks, please contact me.

Our friends miss their nomadic pier.

**(I have also been known to drift aimlessly.)**

# LITTLE MOSQUE ON THE WATER

*A boatload of new Muslim in-laws*

My previous story discussed my friend who had purchased a waterfront home and was afflicted with a wandering wharf. (I'm pleased to report that, after further meanderings following the spring ice break-up, his gypsy jetty was returned home and is now securely fastened to the shore.)

My friend then decided to purchase a motorboat; a vessel worthy of his perambulating pier and capable of providing hours of fun for the whole family.

Determined to avoid any mistakes, he prevailed upon an expert mariner of his acquaintance to accompany him to the boat dealer; a seasoned captain sharp of eye and pooped of deck.

That salty seadog wasn't available, so he chose me instead.

I was honoured by his vote of confidence and mindful of the great responsibility. My wife muttered something about my qualifications, considering my local renown as the Propeller Pranging King.

After boarding several craft at the dealership, I encouraged him to buy the current model of the boat that had proven itself to be a reliable runabout for my family for 10 years.

The sparkling new vessel was duly delivered and the dealer provided my friend with the requisite instructions. I added my own advice, gleaned from years of cruising our lovely Kawartha Lakes, dealing with wind and wave, shoals and sandbars, coves and currents, and indignant topless sunbathers.

My friend, a British immigrant of Anglo-Saxon Protestant vintage, had recently re-married. His new bride, a gracious and elegant refugee from Uganda, is a highly successful business-woman of the Muslim faith. A large extended family became his new in-laws.

Anxious to show off his new boat, eager to impress his new relatives, my friend invited his wife, mother-in-law, brother-in-law and his wife, plus assorted offspring including a four-month-old baby, to join him on the vessel's maiden voyage on Chemong Lake.

The engine roared into life, the lines were cast off, the freshly-minted skipper eased the throttle forward, and the sleek craft slid ahead to cries of joy and admiration. My friend felt like the mighty mariners of his British heritage: famous captains like Nelson, Drake, Cook, and Kawalsky.

He cruised to the centre of the lake and turned, ready to charge down the middle, surely to more adulation from his inaugural passengers.

That's when the engine died.

Despite repeated tries and frantic troubleshooting checks, the engine stayed dead. Actually, the entire electrical system was toast. Burnt toast, in fact.

As a sea of formerly-trusting eyes stared at him, my friend's first thought was: "what a wonderful impression I'm making on my new in-laws."

His next thought was: "I can't wait to throttle the bloody idiot who recommended I buy this boat."

Adding insult to immobility, he had forgotten the bloody idiot's advice to always set sail with that essential piece of modern nautical gear: his cellphone.

No other boat was in sight, to come to their rescue. My friend wondered how long would it take to paddle back to his dock, and would he have enough energy left for a good throttling afterwards?

At that point, his bride calmly reached into her pants pocket and pulled out her cellphone. They called a rescuer, who came out in his boat and towed them back home, my friend fuming at the ignominy of it all.

The dealer's mechanic later discovered the problem was an electrical short, a rare "new boat" glitch. However, my friend knew the real problem; he had violated the First Rule of Seafaring:

Take not a Bloody Idiot to a Boat Sale.

***(I have lots more free nautical advice.)***

# NOT A TEDDY BEARS' PICNIC

*Dumb luck saved their lives*

A friend, raised in Northern Ontario who today operates a successful business there, told me this adventure of youthful entrepreneurship and sheer dumb luck. (Names have been changed for reasons which will soon become obvious.)

When he was 12, Jean Pierre (JP) concocted a unique way to make money. He led other kids to the town dump and, for five dollars, gave them a close encounter with wild black bears.

The bruins came every evening to rummage for food. Beforehand, JP led his paying customers inside a derelict van in the centre of the dump.

To attract the hungry bears, he smeared honey on the window sills. The hidden urchins watched in silent awe as the animals lumbered up and licked off the honey.

When the kids were ready to go, JP threw lit firecrackers out of the van. The bears fled at the explosions and so did the kids, in the opposite direction.

This went on for many profitable nights. Then his clients grew bored, so JP, a consummate hustler, devised something new:

For five bucks each, JP bet that he and his younger brother, Henri, could scale a tree and remain perfectly safe. The other kids, knowing that black bears are excellent climbers and anticipating hopefully-bloody mayhem, accepted the wager.

Several trees grew in the dump. JP selected a young narrow birch, reasoning that it was too thin to support a bear's weight. With the van jammed with eager voyeurs, JP and Henri shinnied up the tree before the bruins arrived.

Seven bears foraged for fast food below the treed boys. Not one looked up. JP silently exulted at all the cash that would soon be his.

Then, for the first time, two cubs appeared. To everyone's shock, they ascended a spruce next to the boys' birch perch. When they reached the same height, both pairs of cubs, two with fur and two without, gawped at each other.

The furry cubs let out an alarmed squeal. Their mother charged over and skidded to a halt beneath the spruce, looking for the source of her cubs' distress. Eventually, she looked up the birch, straight into the boys' terrified eyes. JP still remembers those angry brown eyes boring into his.

Mama bear let out an enraged bellow and proceeded to climb the birch. Henri, who was below JP, let out his own bellow and proceeded to climb over his brother. He succeeded, but mama kept sliding back to the ground. JP's theory about the tree being too thin was right.

Then mama bear started pushing against the birch, shaking it violently. Panicked, JP considered two options.

Option A: throw Henri down, and as the beast chased him, JP could escape.

Option B: activate his failsafe plan, although it meant losing the bet.

He selected Option B; if it didn't work, he could always throw Henri down later.

As the tree swayed dangerously and the boys held on for dear life, JP yelled for his other brother, Claude, who was in the van, to light and throw the firecrackers.

"I can't!" Claude screamed back. "I don't have the matches!"

JP cursed. Where were the damn matches?

He felt his pants pocket. He had the damn matches.

Henri shouted he couldn't hold on much longer, and JP knew Option A would soon not be needed.

Suddenly, the two cubs climbed down and scampered off into the woods. With a final mighty shake of the birch, and a disgusted snort, mama followed her offspring.

JP and Henri clambered down, paid off their bet, and went home to change their underwear.

*(I have only had bare encounters. One is on page 164.)*

# WHERE, OH WHERE DID OUR YCRY GO?

*The Circle of Life in neighbourhoods*

Neighbourhoods are living organisms. They evolve and change over the years, for better or worse.

Humans are living, evolving organisms too and, like neighbourhoods, they only grow in one direction: old. (Okay, some of us also tend to grow out.)

My neighbourhood has seen a lot of changes in recent years. Many long-time residents have sold their homes and moved away. New younger families have bought those homes and moved in.

Without any warning whatsoever, much less written permission from existing residents, our neighbourhood now has a large crop of young children scurrying around.

My wife and I looked at all these YCRY (Young Couples with Rambunctious Youngsters) enveloping us, and we realized something quite shocking: We used to be one of those YCRY.

Over two decades ago, we moved here when our son was just two years old. Our yard resembled many of our neighbours' yards at that time: toys of all sizes and shapes, wading pool, sandbox, tree swing, basketball net, and some stuff for the kid, too.

When did our YCRY status get usurped? How did we transform from YCRY into MacWAS (Middle-aged couple With Adult Son)? Nobody asked our permission. We never signed any document. We were completely blindsided.

(And somebody sped up our calendar, too. The years don't last a full 12 months anymore; it now seems like a year goes by in six weeks.)

Some of our remaining older neighbours have it even worse than us: they have transformed into MacWOG (Middle-aged couple With - Omigod! - Grandchildren). And their yards once again resemble those of the YCRYs. (Proving that it's never wise to have garage sales of stuff your kids outgrow, because you'll surely need it again. And don't even think of trading in that mini-van for a sports car, either.)

All this demonstrates that the eternal Circle of Life also occurs in neighbourhoods: young becomes old, is replaced by young and a Tim Horton's, and the cycle begins anew. The only constants are lawn mowers, laundry, chasing after the garbage truck and banks profiting from hefty mortgages.

However, some people fail to recognize that neighbourhoods go through cycles. As our area went through its most recent change, another transformation occurred because of short-sighted tax-hungry bureaucrats.

For decades, our rural neighbourhood had a charming piece of greenspace, designated by the township as a park. Though it had no playground equipment, or ball diamond, or even a township employee to regularly cut the grass (the adjoining neighbours did it), that park ably served the kids who grew up around it. It was a safe place to play all sorts of ball games, chase butterflies, fly kites, set off fireworks, have neighbourhood corn roasts, and let one's dog have a good romp.

Then, after everyone's offspring had grown, our "civil servants" quietly declared our little grassy common "underused" and therefore "surplus land". It was swiftly sold off to the highest bidder, a house was promptly constructed, and a very nice YCRY took up residence therein.

As a supreme irony, that YCRY family was the vanguard of many that have since moved in over the past two years. Our neighbourhood now has a host of YCRYs, along with many MacWOGs - with no park to play in.

Despite meddling bureaucrats, most neighbourhoods are resilient, self-perpetuating eco-systems full of hard-working friendly people. Though I'm still confused as to how my wife and I lost our YCRY status.

*(Our yard still has lots of toys and I may eventually let our son play with them.)*

# FELINE FOLLIES

*Which are smarter: cats or dogs?*

There is an age-old argument about which is smarter: cats or dogs.

Some say it's dogs, since they're so trainable, especially for essential duties, like service dogs for the disabled, sniffer dogs for drugs or explosives, rescue dogs for buried victims, guard dogs, hunting dogs, lap dogs, and those very special dogs that prevent frustrated authors from committing suicide.

Others claim cats are smarter, because they're able to perfectly train their human servants to feed them at regular intervals, to tolerate their disgusting fur balls, and to buy nice furniture that is ideal for scratching.

Heck, in ancient Egypt, cats were even worshiped as gods. That never happened to dogs.

Here is more compelling evidence which demonstrates that felines can outshine fidos.

Our long-time friend (who's known my wife since conception) related this story of her father-in-law's cats and dog (the latter borrowed from our friend for a week that became forever). All names have been changed to protect yours truly.

Soon after Abbott, the purloined pooch, arrived at the father-in-law's farm, a kitten, named Costello, joined the existing cat menagerie; a much-needed reinforcement to help keep the local mouse population in line. Abbott tolerated Costello as an inescapable annoyance (long-married wives can relate to this).

After Costello had matured into a cat, she established herself as an excellent mouser. Yet she was disturbed by the sight of the affable Abbott loafing about the farm, while she earned her keep.

So the cat decided to teach the mutt how to catch mice.

She trained Abbott as she would a kitten, presenting him with a freshly-caught yet still alive rodent, then pinning said rodent by its tail against the floor with one paw while batting it to death with the other paw.

The cat was patient with the dog, repeating the scenario again and again until Abbott finally got the message. Then, to their humans' incredulity, the pooch started catching mice on his own.

Now, one could argue that the old dog was smarter, because he learned new tricks. However, other folks insist the cat showed superior brainpower, because it not only believed Abbott had the ability to learn the task, but had the tenacity to teach him.

Regardless, Abbott and Costello became renowned mousebusters.

That farm had other cats: two haughty Siamese named Death and Taxes, and a feline christened Xerox, a true copycat who perfectly duplicated other animals' sounds. In fact, it was Xerox's mimicking skills that first brought him into the family.

It was a dark and stormy night (what a unique opening phrase for a novel!), and the family heard a dog barking at the back porch. Opening the door, expecting to find a wet Abbott, they were astonished to see a thoroughly-soaked cat of indeterminate heritage. Who then proceeded to enter the dry warm house and take command, as cats were put on this planet to do.

Besides barking like a dog, Xerox could imitate many other sounds. He could perfectly emulate the distinctive yowl of the two Siamese, which came in handy when he caused a mess or broke something. He would yowl as he scampered away, leaving his human lackeys to blame Death and Taxes (something we've been complaining about for centuries).

When he wanted to be let out of, or into, the house, he barked like Abbott until his humans came and opened the door.

Personally, I think cats and dogs are equally dumb. After all, they both lick themselves.

*(I am not owned by cat or dog. I'm indentured to a wife.)*

# 20,000 LEAGUES
# UNDER KATCHAWANOOKA

### *Strange sights mystify the locals*

This area is afflicted with Wandering Dock Syndrome. (Refer to my earlier story about friends' gypsy jetty on Chemong Lake.)

The disease has now spread to Katchawanooka Lake.

Owners of a charming cottage resort north of the village of Lakefield, Ontario, were distressed last January when their swim platform took advantage of the strong current caused by unseasonably high water to go sightseeing. Dragging its anchor, the platform slowly crept off towards vivacious Lakefield.

Beth and Barney, the innkeepers (not their real names), faced a quandary: their boat was snug in winter storage. How could they rescue their truant floating lumber?

Then Barney had one of his Great Ideas. He'd simply tow the thing back home by walking along the lake bottom.

A certified scuba diver, Barney had traded 2,000 perfectly good dollars for a dry suit, to keep him toasty in frigid waters. The lake water in winter was a balmy 40 degrees Fahrenheit. Barney couldn't understand why his dive buddies declined to join him on his rescue mission in such ideal conditions.

(To some Canadian divers, any water that isn't completely stiff is ideal conditions.)

Still, if he waited until spring for the water to warm up, their dock would be halfway down the St. Lawrence River. So Barney misplaced a cardinal rule - never dive alone - and went solo.

(He cheerfully admits his IQ tends to be smaller than his shoe size (12) when it comes to physical challenges.)

Donning the suit and the rest of his scuba gear, minus the fins, he packed extra lead onto his weight belt, inflated his suit and Buoyancy Compensator (BC) with air, and entered the lake. The current floated him downstream to their perambulating platform.

Once at the dock, he deflated both suit and BC and sank like a stone along the platform's anchor line to the murky bottom 20 feet below. He then picked up the 50-pound anchor and laboriously trudged against the robust current back up the lake, following the anchor's drag marks along the bottom.

He walked in slow motion: body leaning forward, boots raising lazy puff-clouds of dark mud. It was eerily reminiscent of the underwater walkabout of Captain Nemo and his crew in Disney's classic *20,000 Leagues under the Sea.* Minus the *Nautilus.* And the giant squid.

It was hard work. The cold water, heavy anchor, weight of the massive platform against the current, all caused our Canadian Cousteau to huff and puff through the regulator clenched between his numb lips. He sounded like Darth Vader doing the Olympic Marathon. Apart from the bubbles.

His air supply dwindled rapidly.

Finally reaching the right spot, he jammed the anchor among some rocks and, exhausted, started lumbering shoreward.

But his adventure wasn't over yet.

Somehow, the anchor or its chain had caught the clasp on his weight belt. He suddenly lost his belt and bobbed to the surface, where the current swept him downstream.

He eventually managed to come ashore, walking soggily and half-frozen through a homeowner's yard to the road, and then clumping back home, still in full scuba gear.

Local residents, already amazed at seeing a dock move upstream against the current and re-anchor itself, were completely flummoxed when they later found mysterious size 12 deep footprints in the snow leading away from the water.

They fear that the fabled Wanooka Monster has sprouted legs and come ashore. A posse is now patrolling the lakeshore, armed with shotguns and nets. Please keep the truth to yourself. Look how stories about the Loch Ness Monster boosted tourism in Scotland. Why not here?

Nessie, meet Nookie.

*(I firmly believe a monster also lives in our backyard pond.)*

# Chapter Three

## Living

# "HELLO,
# I'M FROM THE GOVERNMENT"

### *The phone survey from hell*

Federal legislation has discouraged many bothersome telemarketers, thereby leaving the field open for something even worse, as this true story illustrates:

We were eating dinner, jazz music partially overcoming the perpetual frenzied barking of the psychotic dogs in the neighbour's yard, when the phone rang.

My wife answered while I quickly swiped food from her plate. She heard a lethargic female voice claiming to represent Statistics Canada. We had been randomly selected to participate in a community survey on health care. Participation was voluntary.

Seeing her dinner almost gone, my wife sighed, pulled up a chair, and settled in with her wine glass and her feet up to do her civic duty. The interviewer asked who else was in the house, and my wife identified a food vacuum of the husband variety. The interviewer said she'd rather talk to me. Annoyed, my wife gave me the phone. I asked how long would this survey take?

"Oh, 20 to 40 minutes, depending on your medical history," said the voice, with the smug tone of a chronic complainer sitting next to you on an eight hour sold-out flight, knowing you are well and truly trapped.

"That's an outrageous amount of time, and damn presumptuous besides," I said. "Medical matters are confidential between a person and their doctor, assuming you're lucky enough to have one these days." I hung up. We thus entered a new level of hell in Dante's Inferno.

The phone rang the next night, at exactly the same time. My wife again answered. StatsCan asking for me.

She told the bureaucrat that I had no interest in taking their intrusive survey, and offered her input instead. The caller declined.

This process was repeated the following evening. And the evening after that.

We discovered that once StatsCan "randomly" selects you for a "voluntary" survey, you have as much chance of saying "no" as a groom with a shotgun jammed into his back.

After two weeks of this productive expenditure of taxpayer dollars, the calls stopped. We reveled at the cessation of hostilities.

Several days later, an official form letter arrived from StatsCan. Ostensibly signed by a senior bureaucrat, the letter was carefully addressed to "householder" and began with the personalized salutation: "Dear Madam or Sir". It acknowledged that we did not wish to participate in their survey, stated that we had been randomly selected and our participation was voluntary - and ended with a promise that the interviewer would call again.

I promptly faxed off a reply, noting that Madam was willing to participate, but she had not been good enough for the interviewer. Sir was not willing. So unless they changed their sexist bureaucratic minds and accepted the input of Madam, please stop bothering us. With a flourish, I signed it: "Bruce Householder".

Several days later, the phone rang. Hopeful that it was a friend, relative, or even a carpet cleaning company working our neighbourhood, my wife grabbed the receiver.

StatsCan. Asking for me.

My wife said I had sent a letter declining my participation; the caller said she would make a note in my file. (I had a file now!) They still refused her input. They called again the next night.

To halt this insanity, I suggested my wife tell them I just died of Telephonic Stress Disorder. However, she reasoned my death would cause problems with my passport renewal.

Instead, we let our answering machine screen all calls. For three weeks, at about the same time each night, an anonymous caller gave an exasperated sigh and hung up without saying a word.

Then the harassment stopped. Our uncivil servants had likely "randomly" selected another household to persecute.

Unless they're just trying to fake us out.

*(Excuse me. The phone's ringing.)*

# OUT OF THE HAMPER

*It's true! Men can do the family laundry*

These days, everyone's coming out of the closet: gays, lesbians, vegetarians, philatelists. I figure it's time for me to "come out" as well. Out of the hamper in the closet, to be precise. So here goes:

I do laundry.

It's actually a family tradition - on my father's side, of course. My dad did it, I do it, and one day so might my son. (Don't snort, guys; remember your college days when you - eventually - washed your clothes? It didn't affect your masculinity and likely saved your social life.)

When we were just married, and negotiating responsibilities in our new partnership, my bride couldn't believe her good fortune to discover I enjoyed doing the laundry. She immediately agreed that would become one of my duties; in exchange, she even accepted cleaning bathrooms.

Still, when I first disappeared with her things into the laundry room, she was as nervous as I was sitting down to her first meal. It turned out that my surprise at her excellent culinary skills mirrored hers at seeing her clothes come back all the same size and colours.

I admit to some trepidation laundering her stuff at first. Her outfits were constructed of mysterious fabrics and some seemed quite flimsy. Then there were the "unmentionables"; lacy things like those on certain Sears catalogue pages eagerly scrutinized by pubescent boys. All of which I'd never washed before, having been a bachelor rarely into cross-dressing.

Today, thirty years later, my wife couldn't wash clothes to save her life; she proudly boasts that she doesn't even know how to turn the machine on.

I, on the other hand, have laundry down to a highly-organized art: separate piles of similar clothing, with each pile washed when it reaches a certain height, ensuring an environmentally-conscious full tub and a regular supply of clean togs.

With most guys, their "sanctum sanctorum" is the den or workshop. With me, it's the laundry room, and no females allowed. My wife's girlfriends are so envious, they could just spit.

But it hasn't all been lemon-freshness. We've had to deal with societal stereotypes. For example, when we shop for a new washer, the salesperson automatically starts yakking at my wife about the features, and can't understand why she looks bored and eyes the stoves across the aisle.

Meanwhile, ignored, I'm all over the machine, examining everything. The more dials and buttons it has, the better (it's a male thing). And if it comes with chrome highlights and racing stripes, consider it sold.

If a new laundry detergent is being flogged at our local supermarket, my wife expertly stick-handles the free sample huckster over to me, flummoxing the person into forgetting her canned patter.

Most guys attempting laundry the first time, usually ruin anything less than 24 oz. double-rivetted cattle-drive-tough denim, resulting in their permanent banishment from the washing machine.

Which is probably what they wanted anyway.

To encourage a more equitable workload between couples, and as a public service to laundrophobic men, here are my secrets to sudsing success:

First: *always read the label.* It should have the washing instructions in both official languages (English and symbols). However, if the label only has symbols, make no attempt to decipher them unaided, otherwise you'll go mad. If you can still find it, the user's manual that came with your washing machine should have a chart that translates what the symbols mean. Failing that, you'll have to ask a professor of hieroglyphics.

More tips: *always* separate colours from whites, use cold water, and hang-dry whenever possible. "Hand wash" means use the Delicate Cycle (her frillies go into a mesh bag that's sold in the "intimates" (women's underwear) section of department stores.

Have your honey go in to buy it for you.).

"Colour-fast" is a sick practical joke, and "wrinkle-free" is optimistic. Stain-remover spray is your secret weapon. And if it says "dry clean only", trust me: they're really serious.

Although few women would agree, I find doing laundry quite relaxing: a mundane yet essential task demanding focussed organizational skills. Logistics Management at its finest.

But I don't do ironing.

*(Actually, nobody in our family does ironing.)*

# BEWARE TROJAN HORSES

*Inventions that promised to make our life easier*

I'm always wary of the latest invention that promises to "make our life easier". These claims reverberate throughout history, yet we never learn.

Millennia ago, when Cavewoman Og invented the wheel (to facilitate her escape from her mate's Wednesday Poker Night), it was hailed as a wonderful improvement, saving our hairy ancestors from dragging everything around.

Yet, by enabling the auto to be mobile, the wheel actually increased our stress levels. Ever had to change a flat tire in the rain? Or cope with a carload of restless squabbling kids on a long drive?

Og's round invention also led to the creation of the wheelbarrow, causing gardening and landscaping chores, ruining many a lazy weekend. Furthermore, it encourages in-laws to visit far more frequently than tolerable.

The automobile itself was praised as one of the greatest of modern inventions, resulting in many beneficial spin-offs like lovers' lanes and fast-food drive-through windows. However, the car also set our blood pressure soaring: traffic jams, repair bills, insurance, back seat drivers, starting it on frigid Canadian mornings, and loaning it to our teenagers.

Indoor plumbing freed our forefamilies from using cold, drafty outhouses and bathing in big tin tubs in the centre of the kitchen. Yet indoor plumbing also increased our daily tension. Just ask a large family with only one bathroom, early any weekday morning. But don't try to cut in line.

It created a marital conflict that didn't exist with rustic outhouses: who cleans the bathroom(s)?

Thanks to Wilbur and Orville, airplanes became popular, shortening long trips and providing employment for pilots, flight attendants, baggage manglers, and purveyors of bland alien food served in tiny containers. But humankind's stress levels climbed along with planes' takeoff angles. Delayed flights. Missed connections. Luggage sent to exotic foreign destinations - or lost entirely - while you land in Moose Jaw. Airlines going bankrupt just before your eagerly-awaited and pre-paid vacation starts.

Yet the inventions keep on coming. Cell phones, which liberated us from enslavement to land-line phones and the trauma of being unreachable when we ventured away, also amplified our mental anguish. Like being in an area of no service when you need it most. The battery dying in the middle of an important conversation. The monthly bill arriving with extra fees the seller neglected to mention.

Even doing the laundry has become stressful, thanks to the dizzying varieties of today's detergents: cold water, warm water, dirt fighter, bleaching agent, softener, for colours, for darks, for whites, for confused greys, lemon scented, morning fresh, evening fog, powder, liquid, phosphate-free, soap-free, fortified with iron and nine essential vitamins.

However, all this pales beside the most diabolical invention ever, the one most touted as making our lives easier: the computer. No device ever created causes more stress. Nothing turns the air bluer at the office or in the home, than people swearing at their computer.

As if the infernal thing could hear them. (Actually, it can; it just doesn't care.)

Computer use is directly proportional to increased Valium use in modern society. Computer-generated statistics prove it.

For myself, I've coped with computers by adopting a zen-like outlook. They're cool if I stay cool. Live and let live. Peace, man.

Oh, I just heard the funniest joke ever, guaranteed to make even Ebenezer Scrooge laugh. Let me keyboard it into my laptop here before I forget it:

There was this naked **ERROR-ERROR-SYSTEM-MELT-DOWN-HAH-HAH----**

*(I'm now shopping for medication and a new laptop.)*

# TWO WORDS THAT GUARANTEE A HAPPY MARRIAGE

*Be very careful how you say them*

Having celebrated our (gasp!) 30th wedding anniversary, we are often asked what is our secret. How have we managed to buck the national divorce trend to stay happily married after three decades?

Depends who you ask.

My wife would tell you it's because of love, or how we make each other laugh, or compatibility, or because she hides my car keys so I can't escape when she's not looking.

While I'd certainly agree with all that (especially the last one), I would tell you that, for husbands, the secret to a happy marriage is two simple words:

"Yes, dear."

Now, these two words are not new. They've been in use among couples since Adam and Eve went looking for a preacher. The secret is in *how* men use these wonderful words. Amazingly versatile, the words can have different meanings simply by altering the tone of your voice. Some examples:

Said in a careful non-committal tone, "yes, dear" is a safe response to those tricky questions that women, compelled by mysterious biological urges, abruptly ask, like: "should I change my hair style?" or "do you think I need a new outfit?"

In a tone of mild irritation, "yes, dear" is a socially-acceptable response to her completely-unfair public commands, such as at a restaurant ("Please stop eating off my plate") or on a bus ("Please get off my lap and stand holding the bar").

Other handy, time-tested response tones:

**Shame:** "You mean you ate *all* the leftover casserole? There was enough left for two more meals!" (Helpful hint: as you mumble "yes, dear", hang your head down; it helps portray sincere contrition.)

**Excitement:** "My God! We have 30 minutes to ourselves. Shall we go upstairs?" (Do look up from the TV and nod eagerly as you say "Yes! Dear!")

**Resignation:** "My mother is coming to stay with us, sweetheart. For two months." (Force a smile as you grit out "yessss, dear". Do not, under any circumstances, cringe.)

**Deniability:** "If you were at a business meeting all afternoon, why is this golf course receipt in your pants pocket?" (Say "yes, dear?" in a tone of befuddlement, as perfected by those federal bureaucrats caught in the Liberal sponsorship scandal.)

**Authority:** "Shall we watch that lingerie special on TV tonight?" (Deep voice: **YES. DEAR.**)

However, be very careful to use the appropriate inflection at all times. You're headed for the marriage counsellor if you use the resignation tone in response to "shall we go upstairs?".

And beware! To check if we males are really paying attention, women sometimes ask Wrong Questions, usually during the crucial final minutes of a close playoff game. Consider the awful consequences of responding with a distracted "yes, dear" in answer to: "do you think I'm getting fat?" or "do you think she's pretty?"

Incidentally, "yes, dear" only works for males. If your honey says "yes, dear", it means she's only agreeing to something just to shut you up (she'd really rather be doing anything else, even cleaning toilets). Or she's buttering you up for some appalling chore, like watching Oprah with her.

Some readers may accuse me of copping out, of sidestepping an animated discussion or the revelation of true feelings, by simply uttering "yes, dear".

Well, to that I say:

"Yes, dear."

(You can't argue with 30 happy years together, bub.)

Happy Anniversary, sweetheart.

*(I once said "yes, dear" to a Wrong Question: "would you like to help me shop for shoes?" Oh, the horror, the horror.)*

# THIS IS A JOB FOR
# CYBER SLEUTH

*Be wary of what you overhear*


I only caught part of the conversation between the two men in the noisy coffee shop, but it was enough.

One man said: "I saw her on the Internet. Her photo was beautiful - lovely legs - and her description said she's a filly who could do anything and is very quiet and willing."

His buddy replied: "Wow, sounds great! You gonna arrange a meeting?"

"Dunno. The wife was cruising the Net herself and found a listing for a nice stud. His photo really showed off his muscles. His listing read: "20-year-old gentleman looking for a good home. Very healthy and an easy keeper. Ready to be anything you want him to be."

"Huh. That must make you a little jealous."

"Yeah. I thought the wife was satisfied with what she had. But if I get myself a new l'il filly, in all fairness, she deserves to get herself a new stud."

"Yep, fair is fair."

I couldn't believe my ears. These guys were obviously talking about some Internet site for male and female prostitutes. Either that or mate swapping. And they had the nerve to discuss it in a public place!

Then one man asked for the web site address. I strained to hear it, but I only caught the last part: "incanada.com".

As a good citizen, I fully intended to alert the police about this web site of debauchery - after I checked it out myself, just to be sure it existed. Didn't want to waste the cops' time on a hoax. I think that's an offense.

Returning home, I pried the teenager off the family computer.

(When I speak, he listens. This time, I guaranteed superb hearing with the keys to the car and $20 to see a movie with his lady friend.)

I then ensured my better half was occupied for an hour ("Hon, you should watch Oprah today; her guest is a man who cooks, cleans, does laundry and always puts the toilet seat down. Oprah's going to raffle off some clones of him.").

Then, safely alone and filled with righteous zeal, I searched the Net for that awful site. I used many likely combinations of words ("hookers 'r' us", "exotic escorts", "lascivious ladies"), always ending with "incanada.com".

Nothing.

Finally, I typed in "studs and fillies" and got lucky. My computer binged that a match had been found. Great! I'd write out the full address and call the local constabulary immediately, so they could shut down this electronic den of inequity.

Man, maybe I'd even get a citizen citation! I resolved to be modest at the awards ceremony.

The site came up and I sat stock-still, not even breathing. I'd found it. Just like those two guys had said. Available studs and willing fillies. With photos. Beautifully posed photos. Plus phone numbers and email addresses. The site was hosted right here in bucolic Peterborough, too!

I swallowed hard. My face flushed in embarrassment. Thank goodness I had not told my wife about this! She'd have a few choice words to say!

The web site was "horsesincanada.com". The studs and fillies were actually *horses.*

Well, how was I to know? Anyone could have made the same mistaken assumption.

Then, just before I signed off that site, my eye caught this listing: "Belgians for sale. Lots of brains and quick to learn."

Belgians? Those nice french-speaking Europeans who do wonderful things with chocolate?

Are we *really* talking about horses here?

*(I obviously know nothing about horses and the folks who breed them.)*

# JUST DO IT!

*Long-time couples don't need to ask permission*

The need to ask permission is drummed into us from an early age. We're taught to ask parents for permission to do or take stuff. Then to ask teachers for permission, then our employers, then government authorities. All of which serves a purpose. Our society would degenerate into chaos if everyone simply did as they saw fit, without permission. (Unless they were mega-rich and famous. Or arrogant corporate CEOs.)

However, when two consenting adults are living together in couplehood, especially if they've been doing so for decades, why can't the ritual of asking permission be relaxed, or even abolished? It would save so much time and effort. Self-help gurus are always spouting off about "empowerment"; surely that applies to those blessed with a long-term relationship?

On some privately-owned pleasure boats, you find this sign: "On board, the Captain's word is law, and I have my wife's permission to say so." There's two things wrong with that sign. One, it presupposes the Captain is male. There are many female Captains who are quite competent, and have the lower insurance premiums to prove it (being far less reckless than males). Two, one spouse shouldn't have to get - or give - permission to the other.

Why should a wife always have to ask permission to indulge herself in some well-deserved rewards, like a spa retreat, casino visit, girls' night out, or 18-hour-chick-flick-marathon-and-to-heck-with-housework?

Why should a husband need permission to reward himself with a guys' poker night, fishing trip, pub crawl, or Sunday-afternoon-triple-sports-marathon-on-TV-and-to-heck-with-yardwork?

Couples are supposed to be so sympatico, so on the same

wavelength, that each knows the other's innermost thoughts and feelings, right? Therefore, asking permission is an unnecessary expenditure of precious oxygen that would be far better spent uttering romantic endearments or inventive excuses for not doing chores.

Why ask if you can have that last piece of pie? Just take it. Why ask if you can use the bathroom first? Just march in there.

Why ask if you should buy that expensive evening dress? Charge it, you've earned it. Why ask if you should purchase those pricey golf clubs? Get them (it will balance that expensive evening dress she just bought).

Why ask if your Significant Other would appreciate a getaway weekend in Toronto? Book it, and watch the wonderful surprised look when you display the pair of expensive non-refundable tickets to a five-hour opera.

It's your right to invite your mother to come stay with you for several months, without first asking your spouse if he/she would mind. Your mother is a great conversationalist; why, she has an opinion on absolutely everything. Don't spend hours reaching consensus on redecorating the entire house in the latest trendy fashion. Just do it. Everyone loves surprises.

There's no need to ask if your honey would mind if you traded-in the family van for a two-seater high-performance sports car with no trunk space, that will be paid off when you're 75. Such spontaneity strengthens relationships.

Bring your boss or a gang of your old college buddies home for dinner, without warning. And if it's Leftover Night, so what? Dishes piled high, kitchen an Apocalypse Now? No big deal; adds atmosphere.

If everyone followed my advice, long-term relationships would always have that exciting spark, that constant thrill of life-threatening danger, which keeps the senses sharp and the blood energized.

Now you may wonder: does this obviously-suicidal man, happily married for 34 years, dare to practice what he preaches? I certainly do. Whenever my wife gives me permission.

*(I always do whatever I darn well please - in my dreams.)*

# SNOW AND TELL

## *The dog days of spring*

"Spring is sprung, the grass is riz - oh look at where the dog poop is."

Every spring, as winter's fluffy snow blanket slowly melts, surprises are revealed.

Dog owners already know what to expect. No surprises there. Grimly, they march out onto their lawns to gather in the winter's harvest.

Though not owned by any dog, I always regard spring thaw with a mixture of joy and trepidation. Joy because winter's finally over and summer fun is just around the corner. Trepidation because I'm never sure what that word means, or what I'll find out there once the snow melts.

That beautiful sculpted snow mound in the backyard that looked so artistic during the winter, slowly revealed itself to be that imported lawn ornament that was not made for our sub-zero climate and which we forgot to bring in before that first snowfall last November. Oops.

Our bench on the patio gradually came to light - along with what used to be my best pliers that I'd been looking for all winter, while blaming the wife and son for callously misplacing them. Apology time.

As the snow receded, that vaguely snake-like pattern next to the house became our new garden hose, bought just last summer and not drained and put away like it should have been. Gah.

The cute little bear-like shape by our backyard fountain became emphatically bear-shaped as the white stuff evaporated: our nephew's favourite stuffed bear, now decidedly worse for wear, which he'd left out there during a late-fall visit and which we'd turned our house upside-down looking for once he returned home and tearfully called us.

You'd think the critter would have found a snug cave somewhere.

That series of mysterious lumps on the lawn finally transformed into the metal Tonka construction toys which we'd bought when our son was young and which our friend's young daughter now played with whenever she came over. She'd neglected to return them to the garage. Those Tonkas would never build anything again; rust had fused them into immobility.

Hmm, maybe I'll spray-paint 'em in bold colours and pretend they're lawn ornaments.

The mound of snow filling our patio chair (which hadn't been brought in either) gave us quite a scare. It started to look suspiciously humanoid as it melted. Female humanoid.

My God! My wife's elderly widowed Aunt Perpetua had gone missing last December, and she loved visiting us. Suppose the old dear had arrived while we were away visiting relatives in Montreal, decided to sit in our patio chair until we returned - and froze to death! We had returned in a blizzard; she could have been buried there under the snow all winter!

Several panicked phone calls later, we discovered to our great relief that Aunt Perpetua had reappeared weeks ago (no one had thought to tell us), along with a new husband and other souvenirs of an impromptu Vegas vacation.

Magicians, whether street-corner buskers or David Copperfield, amaze audiences by making things disappear and reappear.

Well, Mother Nature beats 'em all. Her magic cloth of snow makes things quickly vanish, only to rematerialise months later with the speed of a kid forced to eat his vegetables - much to our chagrin.

Hey, that lump over there: is that - could it be - my power drill?

*(I once left myself outside in a blizzard. No one missed me.)*

# OH,
# FOR THE SOUNDS OF SILENCE

*Seasonal insanity, every fall*

Fall is a wonderful time of year here in the Kawarthas.

The crisp crunch of fallen leaves underfoot. The imperious honking of southward-bound tour groups of Canada geese. The ubiquitous whine of leaf blowers.

The carefree chatter of school kids indignant at so much homework. Swimming pools and boats bedecked in their sad winter shrouds. The aromatic smell of wood-burning fireplaces. The annoying whine of leaf blowers.

Cottages being closed up. Convertibles, motorcycles and golf clubs lovingly, regretfully, tearfully placed into storage. Hallowe'en decorations materializing, then morphing overnight into Christmas ornaments. The aggravating whine of leaf blowers.

Shorter days, but more magnificent sunsets. The soothing rustle of leaves in the wind slowly transforming into the barren keen of bare limbs. Baseball-watching giving way to football and hockey fever. The maddening whine of leaf blowers.

The invigorating tang of cool air. Dark rain clouds foreshadowing the future birth of snowflakes. Homeowners tucking away patio furniture and snugly wrapping shrubs in burlap.

The infuriating whine of those leaf blowers!

Carpets of leaves being raked, or mulched, (or ignored in the hope that the wind will blow them onto neighbours' lawns). Storm windows going up. Hanging planters coming down. Garden hoses being drained.

*The demented whine of those leaf blowers!*

The quiet giggle of lovers out for a walk, snuggling together against the chill air. Docks being hauled out of cold water. Water skis trading places with snow skis in garages. Lawn rakes do-si-doing with snow shovels.

THE HOWLING OF THOSE LEAF BLOWERS!

A fresh season of TV. Exciting fall craft shows. Stores bulging with Christmas gifts anxious for a good home. Children already checking out mom and dad's usual hiding places for Christmas presents.

THE WHY-ISN'T-THERE-A-NOISE-BY-LAW-AGAINST-THESE-BLOODY LEAF BLOWERS?!

Scores of women seasonally widowed by husbands disappearing into the bush with gun and beer, answering the primeval Call of Nature. Family-filled Thanksgiving dinners. Election signs competing with For Sale signs on lawns, sometimes electing Her Highness Royal Lepage by write-in votes.

**THOSE I-CAN"T-TAKE-IT-ANYMORE CURSED LEAF BLOWERS!!!**

Early frosts delighting children, scaring vegetable gardeners, and causing frantic early morning searches for car window scrapers. Fall tune-ups. Snow tires excavated from their cobwebbed tombs in dark garage corners.

**THOSE.**

Heavier coats reluctantly exhumed from deep within closets.

**DAMN.**

Winter boots pulled once more into the forefront of shoe trays.

**LEAF.**

Christmas lists being started.

**BLOWERS!!!!**

By now, astute readers will have perceived that leaf blowers annoy me somewhat. When one of them starts up, it's a solo overture which soon grows into an entire orchestra performing a Symphony of Shrieking as others in the neighbourhood join in. A discordant high-pitched caterwaul from hell that goes on for hours. And hours. AND HOURS!

***KREEGAH! Tarzan kill!***

Sorry. I'm better now.

Yes, fall is a very magical time. But, personally, I can't wait for winter with lots and lots of snow. Because with snow, comes silence. The sweet peaceful blessed silence of

**NO MORE LEAF BLOWERS!!!!**

Lovely snow.  Quiet, deep, pristine, beautiful snow.  Peace at last.

Stop.
Listen.
What's that sound?
SNOWBLOWERS??!!

*(I'm now heavily medicated and resting comfortably.)*

# SO MANY CHOICES, SO LITTLE TIME

*The perils of sending a male to buy groceries*

Guys, when She Who Commands sends you to the grocery store - by yourself - for "just a few things", be *very* careful. Especially if you don't usually go shopping.

A case in point:

Her list seemed simple enough. I'd be in and out in ten minutes, tops.

First item: potatoes. A no-brainer. Just grab a bag, heave it into the cart, and move on.

I soon had the same feeling the skipper of the *Titanic* had when he realized his ship had been mortally wounded. I was confronted by a Gourmet Potato display. The lowly spud had become specialized! Four bins each contained different types: Baking, Boiling, Mashing, Roasting. Each bin had its own colour-coded bag, ensuring that when you got home, you could tell a Roasting from a Mashing.

There were three more bins just above, one each for French Frying, Microwave, and Petite Gourmet Boiling.

She had neglected to inform me what she intended to do with the potatoes. Suppose I bought the wrong type? God help us if we mashed a roasting potato by mistake! Or boiled a potato that had been carefully bred for baking! Or deep-fried a microwave spud!

PEI would probably declare war upon Ontario.

(Do they come out of the ground in these seven specialized types, or do highly-trained inspectors determine each spud's proper cooking destiny?)

The ordinary, multi-purpose potato? Several aisles over. But even there I had several choices: white, red, washed, shampooed.

In a quandary, I looked around helplessly. Shoppers were

eyeing me warily, or with looks of pity.

Decisive action was needed. Male honour was at stake.

So I grabbed a bag of each. Filled half the cart.

Well, she never said how many potatoes she wanted, did she?

Okay, next on her list: table salt. That's easy.

Arriving at the salt section, I had that *Titanic* feeling again. Nowadays, when it's time to pass the salt, there's table salt, sea salt (regular and fine), Kosher, coarse, seasoned, iodized, and - I kid you not - gourmet Peruvian Pink and hand-raked fleur-de-sel.

One of each went into the cart.

Next up: bottled water. I discovered there's now five brands of bottled spring water, ten types of flavoured water, three brands with effervescent bubbles, and one for hockey coaches that's fortified with pure Russian vodka.

I couldn't keep putting one of everything into this cart. I had to make a choice sometime.

I picked the one fortified with vodka. Had a feeling I'd need it when I got home.

Things didn't get better. Grocery stores, in their eagerness to please, overwhelm you with specialization in every aisle. Different varieties of tomatoes, lettuce, apples. Endless types of meats, including some that are not meat at all (tofu anyone?). Cookies and cereals and chips in every flavour imaginable. Multitudes of cheeses. Cascades of juices. Bushels of breads.

I was not trained for this.

Yet I refused to emulate other men and call home on the cell phone so she could talk me through it, like Mission Control instructing astronauts on a complicated repair job.

At the check-out, the cashier barely kept a straight face. The guy who loaded the stuff into my trunk guffawed. Twice.

I had one stop left. A simple purchase, for *myself*, without having to choose between a confusing array of specialized types. Nice and easy.

I'll just pop into the mall for a pair of running shoes.

**(*I'm a proud generalist, meaning I can't do anything well.*)**

# NO SEX PLEASE, I'M TOXIC

*A tale of two raccoons with intimacy problems*

This story is about some dear friends; a couple who have been happily married, like, *forever*.

However, since the topic is about intimate relations, our nation's Morality Police and their self-appointed civilian deputies, ever-vigilant guardians of what's naughty and nice for our own good, would have apoplectic fits if it appeared in a general-audience book like this one. (The Corruption Cops overseeing our rural community are still seething over a large colour photo of a sexy woman in fishnets and leather, holding a - gasp - whip, that was published several years ago in our local newspaper, resulting in up to one subscription being angrily cancelled.)

So, instead of my original story, here's a harmless tale about some cute woodland animals. Can't go wrong with that.

Randall Raccoon and his wife, Rutleigh, have been happily married, like, *forever*.

Randy and Rut have three kids and a nice home high in an old oak tree with a mortgage that will be paid off about the time a lasting peace comes to the Middle East.

Then middle age, playing no favourites between human and animal, hit our two furry raccoon friends.

Rut started the roller-coaster of The Change, while hubby Randy developed a chronic disease made inevitable by genetics and a lifestyle that had grown lazy, thanks to a fast-food diet from too many garbage cans.

To control his new ailment, Dr. Owl prescribed powerful medication which Randy had to take for the rest of his life. The meds had a list of possible side effects as long as a politician's excuses, but our raccoon chums discovered a new one:

Randy became toxic to Rut.

Not just during lovemaking, which was certainly bad enough, but even after giving her a nice long kiss. Hyper-allergic to trace elements of Randy's drugs, Rut developed acute burning sensations that only stopped when she kept him firmly at tail's length.

Dr. Owl had never heard of such a thing. It really ruffled his feathers. He suggested Rut had been chewing that funny wildwood weed again. But she had not, and her opinion of Dr. Owl slipped even lower than how she felt about telemarketing chipmunks.

So Randy and Rut consulted Bartholomew Bird and Beatrice Bee. After all, who'd know more about sex than the birds and the bees? Between harvesting worms and making honey, respectively, Bird 'n' Bee considered the Raccoons' problem. They first suggested not kissing ever again, even during sex, which would have been near-impossible anyway since they also said coupling should now done upside-down like opossums.

Rut refused, retorting that they were raccoons, not opossums.

Then they advised Randy and Rut to forsake having intimate relations entirely - after all, they'd had their bandit brood, so why bother? To control their natural urges, the masked varmints were told to take lots of cold showers. Or attend city council meetings.

Still no sale.

Randy started contemplating a celibate, monastic life, like that of Brewster Bear, who'd been living alone in the forest ever since he unexpectedly returned to the den and found his wife and Smoky putting out a fire.

Finally, Bird 'n' Bee suggested kissing like their arctic brethren, by rubbing noses. And for doing what comes naturally, they recommended a complicated procedure involving rose oil, mink fur, sheep's intestine, whipped cream and the jawbone of an elk. Which went over like a drunken hunter with Randy and Rut.

So Randy decided to take matters into his own paws.

He found a new doctor (there's more than one owl in the forest), who prescribed different medication. It worked, and he and Rut went back to making the tree-tops quiver again.

Though they kept using the whipped cream.

*(No animals were harmed in the writing of this story.)*

# HOLD THE PHONE!

*That evil invention torments us still*

Pop quiz: who was the most evil man in history?

Hitler?   Stalin?   Genghis Khan?   Your high school math teacher?

No.

They pale beside the most infamous man of all: Alexander Graham Bell (or that obscure Italian fellow if you believe revisionist historians).

Bell did more damage to humanity than any other man in history. He gave us the infernal device that has plagued civilization ever since:

The telephone.

More powerful than a nuclear bomb, or a nationwide strike, or a spouse's haranguing. Think about it: what else can make a person anywhere on this planet, regardless of country or creed, whether peasant or president, immediately stop whatever they're doing to answer its insistent ring?

What else has the power to halt a face-to-face conversation, whether among friends or with a customer, because you "have to" answer the phone?   You are only granted a small measure of revenge by promptly placing the caller on hold (a practice honed to perfection by large corporations and government bureaucracies).

The fiendish thing has contributed to countless heart and asthma attacks, as people race in from all points of the compass to grab it, panicked at the thought of missing what is surely a vital call ("Hi, we're cleaning carpets in your area this week ...").

Phone calls have been a hitherto-unnoticed cause of our soaring heath care costs.   Ottawa should strike a Royal Commission to study this.

Bell's Bane has destroyed countless harmonious families,

because of its uncanny attraction to teenagers. Teens stick to phones like bills to a credit card. Good luck trying to call home on an urgent matter; the incessant busy signal means your teen has hijacked the phone again. Or is on the Internet, which often operates on a phone line. (If you purchased high-speed cable Internet, foolishly thinking it would free up your phone line, beware: your teen will chat for hours on the phone with the person they're also online with.)

And nothing disrupts family harmony more than when the monthly phone bill arrives. The resulting arguments result in many domestic disturbance complaints - called in, of course.

Phone tyranny has grown beyond Bell's wildest dreams. Not satisfied with the single phone our grandparents suffered with, our parents increased the machine's dominance by placing extensions throughout the house.

Then came the advent of cordless phones, allowing us to carry our tormentor into the great outdoors. Sure it saved us from dashing into the house when the phone rang, but now not only was the peace of our backyards disturbed, but that of our neighbours as well, thanks to our loud conversations.

Then came cell phones, and the gates of perdition were flung wide. Now, for those of us "fortunate" enough to afford one (or two or three - the Family Plan allows the whole family to be enslaved), we can be pestered anytime, anywhere.

Not satisfied with the horror inflicted upon humankind by the telephone itself, Bell's equally-evil descendants developed more diabolical methods of torture: Call forwarding. Call waiting. Call display. Call girls. And the most devilish: corporate voice mail, trapping the hapless for hours in cold electronic labyrinths far more frustrating than the now-extinct bored receptionist.

To add insult to injury: we willingly pay for all this harassment!

What can we do to regain our freedom?

Is the disease too far gone to cure?

I'm not sure. Let's have a conference call to discuss it.

*(As you might guess, I'm constantly hounded, badgered and outfoxed by phone calls.)*

# WHAT YOUR TEEN NEEDS MOST

*An essential item for parents with teenagers*

VCRs and DVDs have one. So do stoves, fridges and microwaves. Cameras and camcorders. Lawn mowers and snowblowers. Cars have one so thick it chokes your glove compartment.

Owner's manuals.

All your important stuff comes with one.

So why, then, don't teenagers? Imagine the blessing for harried parents whose cute 'n' cuddly children morph into The Inscrutable Teen.

An owner's manual would tell you exactly what to do when your teen malfunctions or needs service. Or passes a significant milestone, like turning 19 (legal drinking!), or realizing that they now Know Everything and parents are irrelevant (except for money).

Imagine: no more guesswork! No more calling YOUR parents to ask for advice, which won't work on your teen any better than it worked on you at that age, eons ago.

An owner's manual would tell you how to handle a daughter who proudly introduces her first Serious Boyfriend, who looks like someone you'd run from if you met him in a dark alley. Or even a well-lit one. Someone you instinctively KNOW is bad for your daughter, who'll eventually break her heart. And swipe your beer.

An entire chapter of the manual would be devoted to counselling your distraught teen who's being picked on at school because of how they look, or dress, or act, or the friends they hang out with, or the sports they're not that great at. The chapter would include witty and biting comeback remarks, guaranteed to stun the abusers while motivating them to re-evaluate their harassment and, chastened, promptly join a monastery or convent.

Another chapter would reveal the secret, more sought-after than that legendary alchemist's stone that turned lead into gold, of how to convince your teen to clean up their room and - bonus! - to keep it clean. This chapter would become the most dog-eared one in the entire manual.

You would learn how to gracefully decline their request to borrow the family car and how, when you finally capitulate after the 34,500th request that evening, to guarantee it would be returned washed, waxed, and with a full tank of gas. Without a scratch, of course. A special section would show you how to pre-set the car's top speed at 30 km/h.

Amazed, you would read how to have your teen remember to call you if they're going to be late returning home from an activity, saving you hours of worry.

How to get them to delete countless long-winded messages from their friends off their cell phone's voice-mail, so that you can leave that vital urgent message ("Hon, the house is on fire, I can't find your cat, and your father's run off to Tahiti. Now would be a good time to come home.").

How to limit the hours they spend glued to their computer screen, so they can spend time on that good wholesome stuff you did as a teen. Like watching TV.

How to break them from the habit of ignoring their homework until the absolute last minute, after which frenzied activity accompanied by wails of anguish finally gets it sorta done.

How to counsel them towards a productive, stimulating career for which they're perfectly suited, in your expert opinion, despite their yearning to become something totally weird. Like a politician.

Yes, an owner's manual for your teen would be a Godsend.

Now if only you would read it.

*(My wife and I raised a wonderful son, who managed to survive his teen years and his parents. He refuses to read owner's manuals.)*

# WHAT CHICKEN TASTES LIKE

### *An age-old mystery solved*

This story will answer one of life's Big Questions. How many times have you heard someone say, after tasting an unfamiliar meat: "It tastes like chicken"? How many times have you said that?

My family and I love to travel (especially when creditors are searching for us). During our trips, we always sample the local cuisine of the areas we inflict ourselves upon. We are continually amazed at how many unusual new foodstuffs are first described to us by the locals as "tasting like chicken".

Alligator meat in Florida: "chicken".

Iguana in Grenada: "chicken".

Rattlesnake kebabs in Alberta: "chicken".

Wild goose near the Arctic Circle: "chicken".

Turtle steaks in Barbados. Ostrich kebabs in Aruba. Grilled grouper in the Bahamas. Pulled pork in Georgia. Fresh lobster in Nova Scotia. All supposedly "taste like chicken". (Okay, I was kidding about the lobster. It tastes like heaven.)

In my opinion, the above dishes certainly did not taste like chicken after having eaten them. They all had their own unique taste. Friends who visited Australia ate kangaroo stew and guess what they said it tasted like?

Since people worldwide persist in saying "it tastes like chicken", I can only conclude that chicken farmers must have a powerful lobby group.

Last fall, on a family road trip through our Maritimes and the New England states, we pulled into a quaint roadhouse restaurant in a small New Hampshire town. We knew it was a good place to eat because the parking lot was packed with cars wearing New Hampshire plates.

Once we were seated, a harried waitress eventually came to

our table, admitted she was being run off her feet that night, and took our orders: two Magnificent Meatloaf ("Made with three meats: beef, veal and pork. A carnivore's delight!") for my wife and me and one Classic Country Chicken for our son.

She disappeared into the cacophony of the kitchen. Quite some time later, she re-materialized at our table and safely deposited three precariously-balanced plates.

She vanished before we could tell her that all three dinners were identical.

When she finally reappeared to ask how our meals were, we had almost finished them. I said my son's chicken tasted just like our meatloaf.

She stared at me blankly (I get that a lot), then a horrified look crossed her face as she realized her mistake: our son had ordered the chicken.

She stammered profuse apologies, but we told her to forget it; luckily our son also loved meatloaf and it had indeed been worthy of the title "Magnificent", so no harm done.

Red-faced, she took her leave, still apologizing.

Minutes later, the manager arrived to make his own amends.

"Don't worry about it," said I, a mischievous grin on my ruggedly-handsome features. "Everyone always says this dish tastes like chicken, that dish tastes like chicken. Always made me wonder what chicken itself was supposed to taste like. Well, thanks to your fine restaurant, we now know exactly what chicken tastes like:

"Meatloaf!"

The manager gave me a blank look (See? Told you), then burst into laughter. He thanked us for being good sports about the mix-up, expressed his sympathies to my wife and son for traveling long distances with an obvious goof, and gave our son a free dessert.

So, dear reader, now you know the answer to one of life's Big Questions.

I am now researching the answer to another BQ: on road trips, why am I always left behind at rest stops?

*(You'd never believe where I've been abandoned lately.)*

# SALES BY SYMBOLOGY

*Raptors and panthers and bears, oh my!*

Symbology is part of our daily lives. Not the arcane symbology of the *Da Vinci Code*, but corporate icons.

Animals are big in corporate symbology, especially in the sports world. In hockey, sharks circle penguins, panthers lope after ducks, and coyotes attack bruins. In baseball, four species of birds, plus tigers, diamondbacks, marlins, devil rays and cubs, get territorial with each other. Football critters snarl after squealing pigskins, while all sorts of basketball fauna pound the hardwood, including a resurrected red prehistoric predator with a fondness for wearing tank-tops and shorts.

Animals also lurk in non-sports corporations:

A well-known farm equipment company has a stag, a cereal and a chocolate drink each have hyperactive rabbits, and a famous Italian car company's horse competes head-to-hoof with an equally-famous Italian automaker's bull.

Sheep have been corralled to sell mattresses, with the added ignominy of having big numbers painted on their wooly sides.

In the next pasture, an American automobile manufacturer has branded the ram onto its trucks, while another company lassoed a mustang for its sports car.

A petroleum firm and a cereal company went on safari together and returned with happy tigers to promote their products.

However, in my opinion, this corporate capture of fauna has crossed a line:

Majestic polar bears, those legendary icons of our Canadian Artic, are now sociable drinkers of the world's most famous soft drink, especially at Christmas. Canadians should not take this lying down. Remember, this is the same powerful conglomerate that kidnaped Santa Claus decades ago, redrawing his image and turning him into a corporate shill for their liquid-sugar beverage.

With the polar bear, we are in grave danger of losing something as uniquely Canadian as separation referendums. Also consider the havoc a soft drink diet will cause those bleached bruins: tooth decay, obesity and diabetes. And the most important issue: shouldn't our federal government be receiving royalties?

Yet, it's not just animals being used to make a buck (pun intended).

Leprechauns are peddling cereal. This is a serious matter; those mischievous imps are as Irish as potatoes, pubs and pugilism. Why isn't Ireland protesting?

The lovely Trillium flower, a delight to discover on woodland walks, has been uprooted by the Ontario government as the emblem for all things great and wonderful from our provincial caretakers.

Teddy bears, hugged by children for over 100 years, now entice you to stop at a certain hotel chain for a good night's sleep.

And we must explain to our children that rainbows no longer mean pots of gold, but now symbolize gay and lesbian pride. (Are the leprechauns okay with that, or are they too busy hawking cereal?)

However, the most shocking misappropriation of all, involves the happiest of icons:

To anyone in the Baby Boomer generation, a bright yellow smiley face was a prominent symbol of the 1960s and 70s hippie era: "Have a nice day". Right alongside "Make love not war" and "Don't trust anyone over 30".

Nowadays, it's the symbol for lower prices at the world's largest retailer. Obviously the flower children were too busy exploring reality-altering pharmaceuticals decades ago to bother copyrighting that distinctive face.

The children of the Age of Aquarius used to protest corporate control of our lives. Now they shop with their grandchildren at a big box store that's shanghaied their beloved happy face.

It's enough to make old hippies think they're on a bad trip, man. Especially when that yellow face winks at you.

*(I now don't trust anyone under 30, and I fondly remember the sixties, which means I was never a hippie.)*

# Chapter Four

## On the Job

# I, ROBOT, DEFY YOU

*Artificial Intelligence proves how dumb it can be*

By profession, I'm an association executive: chief administrator of two non-profit organizations. A fast-paced, stimulating career.

Now, association executives are a strange breed. They run their non-profits like a business, except they don't own even the smallest piece of it, and every time a member calls, that's a boss calling (particularly harrowing if your association is very large, with thousands of members).

We administrators are often found on the leading edge: of management techniques, of emerging issues, of technology, (sometimes of a parapet). We have to be that way; the members we serve are either on the leading edge themselves and expect their association to keep up, or they are looking to us to set an example.

In our zeal to be technological leaders, we are quick to use the latest software and mechanical gizmo.

Sometimes too quick.

Several years ago, when voice-recognition software was first introduced, I eagerly embraced it. Instead of dictating my reports and letters, which my assistant would then type while struggling to stay awake listening to my droning voice, this wonderful new software would let me talk directly to my laptop (in a nice way, not the usual cussing). My words would magically appear on-screen, much faster than I could type them using my venerable hunt-and-peck technique, and my computer would only rarely fall asleep. My overworked assistant would be free to do other tasks.

What a time-saver! What a boost to productivity!

I purchased top-of-the-line voice-recognition software and received expert instruction on its use, especially the crucial step of "training" the program to my voice and inflections. I aced all the test modules, producing letter-perfect samples of written material. Ecstatic, I mothballed my dictation equipment and plunged into the world of *Star Trek*.

That's when the trouble started.

With headset on, I dictated several letters. When done, I reviewed what had been transcribed. Good thing I did, too. I was shocked to read what was on the screen.

Every time I had paused in my dictation, whether to reference source material or to gather my thoughts, the software took on a mind of its own. And it wasn't a particularly nice mind, either.

The Artificial Intelligence (AI) apparently grew bored waiting for me to resume speaking, so it added some interesting words to my text to pass the time. "Be bop" and "booby" were sprinkled throughout my paragraphs. During especially long pauses, the spiteful AI strung all three words together: "be bop booby". At one point, an entire sentence of repetitive "be bop booby" appeared, right across the screen.

Instead of saving time, I was forced to locate and edit out all the embarrassing be bops and boobies before giving the disk to my assistant for formatting, lest she thought I had either lost my marbles (always likely), or that I was making improper advances (was my association insured for sexual harassment? Caused by a computer?).

Even being deathly quiet during my pauses, the malevolent automaton typed the offending words. I started having nightmares of vital letters and reports going out with a "be bop" or a "booby" lurking somewhere that both I and my assistant had missed.

I tried everything to correct the malfunction. I talked slower. I talked faster. Louder. Softer. With a suave French accent (I was born and raised in Quebec). I even went back to square one and "retrained" the software, following the instructions of the manufacturer's call centre troubleshooter (who seemed highly amused at my "booby" problem and who smugly informed me that no other user of the software had experienced such a problem. Which made me feel *so* much better).

The problem persisted. My staff developed a theory that the voice-recognition software had recognized me all right: as a dirty-minded pervert.

Then the robotic beast developed a twisted sense of humour.

Finishing dictating a letter to the late Al Palladini, when he was Ontario's Minister of Economic Development, Trade and Tourism, I was horrified at what the machine had written. Instead of "the Honourable Al Palladini", it wrote: "the Honourable Alcoholic Beanie".

Although the minister had a great sense of humour, I was fairly certain he wouldn't appreciate being called an "alcoholic beanie". My name would have been "mud".

The AI had violated the late SF author Isaac Asimov's classic First Law of Robotics: a robot must not allow harm to befall a human, or through inaction, allow harm to befall a human.

That was the last straw.

I stopped using the software (although it still resides in my laptop somewhere, like a cybernetic troll crouching under a virtual reality bridge, doubtless plotting its revenge). I officially labelled the whole thing a failed experiment, while ignoring the giggles of my staff. I reverted to giving my assistant surefire cures for insomnia.

Now, when I do my own typing (such as this article), I use my trusty fingers and not my big mouth. The natural order of the universe is thus preserved.

It also guarantees no more be bops and boobies, saving me from public embarrassment.

Pervert indeed.

*(Bruce beanie Gravel is President be bop of the Ontario Accommodation Association, Peterborough, and Secretary-Treasurer booby of the Tourism Federation of Ontario.)*

# THE SEA WOLF

### *The night an adult timber wolf went downtown*

When I was young, so much younger than today (thanks, Beatles), I took a college course near Montreal that involved timber wolves.

I was at that fearless and stupid age, ideal for jumping out of airplanes (skydiving), communing with sharks (scuba diving) and riding one's motorcycle through Montreal rush hour traffic (suicide).

So when the college asked for a student to "work closely" with a just-captured adult male wolf, I promptly volunteered.

I discovered "closely" meant getting in the cage with him.

Luckily, my professor's prediction proved to be accurate: the wolf was more scared of me than I of him. So I felt other folks should see that the fairy tale of The Big Bad Wolf was just that.

My girlfriend and I were avid divers, and I was in charge of netting interesting speakers for our scuba club's monthly meetings. I decided to haul in a timber wolf.

Some club members wondered at the connection between scuba diving and wolves. I said sharks were often called "wolves of the sea", so understanding wolves would surely lead to comprehending sharks a little better. They wondered if I had "rapture of the deep" (nitrogen narcosis).

Our club met at the Downtown Montreal YMCA. My prof came along, to speak to the members. (Wolves are poor public speakers. When they get bored with an audience, they eat them.) A mostly-housebroken, people-tolerant adult female from the college's wolf pack accompanied us.

We commandeered an ancient college van. To keep her calm, I rode in back with the she-wolf, who answered to the name of Aurora. When she felt like it.

She should have been called Stinky, because she certainly was.

As we left the suburban college and rattled off towards Montreal, the prof announced that Aurora had a bad habit of drooling and was prone to car sickness. My girlfriend, safe in her seat up front, sniggered.

We arrived without incident, except for drool splotches on my jeans. Holding firm to her chain, I walked Aurora down a busy Montreal sidewalk to the front doors of the Y.

I discovered one doesn't walk a wolf; the wolf walks you. Aurora was quite strong and not prone to dawdling.

As we approached the Y, an old drunk hollered: "That's one big dog with some big teeth, buddy!"

I said she was a timber wolf. The drunk's eyes popped wide, his mouth fell open, and he screamed.

We caused quite a commotion as we swept through the lobby of the Y and loped up the stairs (four at a time for her, half that for me) to the meeting room, which was packed with divers and media.

The noisy crowd agitated Aurora, so the prof hurriedly shut her in a big dimly-lit storage closet to chill out - along with me, now majoring in Wolf-sitting.

There I stayed, squatting face-to-snout with my smelly guest of honour, while the prof delivered her speech. When she wasn't pacing back and forth, displaying long wet canines and even longer wetter tongue, Aurora banged into me, hard, obviously reproaching me for dragging her into this mess. Though she had done the dragging.

Just as I was wondering when she had been fed last (she had started licking her chops), the door opened and we were released from captivity. The crowd, much quieter now, ooed and aahed over Aurora.

It was the most popular meeting the club had all year.

However, when I said I would like to work with grizzlies next, the club president appointed another meeting planner.

*(I once answered the Call of the Wild, but it was a wrong number.)*

# MY TIME AS A WOMAN

## *Water and Kleenex don't mix*

In antediluvian times, before personal computers and colour TV, when I was in my teens and had a body that was attractive to girls, I spent two summers as a lifeguard and swimming instructor at an outdoor pool. Mid-way through each summer, to relieve the awful tedium of staring at skimpy bathing suits all day, we lifeguards hosted a Fun Day at the pool. Free admission, free eats and pop, organized games for the children, the works. The festivities were capped by the bravest - or silliest - lifeguards going off the high diving board wearing the most outlandish outfits.

My first year there, I did a "Mary Poppins". Holding the huge umbrella that usually shaded a lifeguard chair, and dressed in an ankle-length thick rubber sou'wester raincoat, hat, and calf-high galoshes, I lumbered off the high board to squeals of laughter.

And almost drowned.

I hit the water with a mighty splash and plummeted straight to the bottom. And stayed there.

No one told me how heavy rubber raingear would be underwater, especially with galoshes full of water.

I tried to swim to the surface, but it was like swimming through thick mud. Realizing I wasn't getting anywhere, and that none of my highly-trained co-workers felt like diving in to demonstrate their rescue skills, I fumbled with the many clasps holding the coat and boots closed.

I finally got out of the raingear and surfaced, gasping. No one had missed me.

The following year, I wanted a less-hazardous outfit. My mischievous girlfriend suggested dressing as a woman. She even volunteered her mother's black one-piece bathing suit, which was the height of fashion - in the 1930s.

I balked, afraid of looking ridiculous. My honey reminded me of how I had looked last year.

"But, a woman's bathing suit!" I protested.

"Why not? Besides, you have great legs. And they'll look even better once we shave them."

"WHAT!?"

"It's all or nothing, lover. Your armpits, too."

Well, I knew the guys on the swim team shaved their bods to get that extra millisecond of speed, and still dated girls afterwards, so I finally agreed.

Ouch. What women go through! (Good thing it was a 1930s bathing suit, so I didn't need a bikini wax.)

Later, putting on the bathing suit, I emulated under-endowed teenage girls everywhere, and stuffed Kleenex into the bra section. Used a whole box. Really filled out the superstructure.

Adding waterproof lipstick donated by a synchronized swimmer, and a gaudy floral bathing cap also swiped from my future mother-in-law, I was a sight to behold as I slowly sashayed up the ladder and out along the high diving board.

Gales of laughter from the kids. Whistles and catcalls from my co-workers. Several requests for a date.

Off the board I went. But I had mis-calculated again. This time, about what would happen to a pound of Kleenex suddenly encountering water at high speed.

I went from a 44D to a 00 in a second, as the Kleenex padding exploded out the top of my top. Dolly Parton instantly became Twiggy.

I surfaced amidst a large cloud of white, soggy tissue. Which slowly sank to the bottom of the pool.

Climbing out, I was confronted by our furious maintenance man, who informed me that he was not going to clean that mess up, no matter how nice my damn legs looked.

For weeks afterwards, the female lifeguards teased me about how nice I'd look in nylons and a mini-skirt. Obviously jealous.

*(I almost never dress in women's clothing anymore. My wife has photos of the above incident, and will gleefully show them to anyone, free of charge.)*

# WHY
# RESTAURANTEURS GET GREY

### *That's not a kilt!*

I have a deep admiration for people working in the hospitality industry, because of the many different types of customers they encounter. Most patrons are great, but there's a minority that make folks contemplate a career change.

This is especially true for restauranteurs, who occasionally must deal with diners who are rude, or difficult to please, or inebriated, or messy, or cheapskates with the gratuity.

Sometimes all of the above.

But enough about me.

This tale was related to me by Gordon and Amy, the charming owner/operators of one of Peterborough's finest Greek restaurants. (Their names have been changed to protect my dessert.)

Before returning to our fair city, where they grew up, Gordon and Amy operated two Greek eateries, in secession, in Toronto. Their last restaurant had a regular customer named Sam.

Now Sam was a big, tall man, who always dressed well when he dined there. He was also rather eccentric (somewhat like your humble scribe). Yet he never caused trouble and was always courteous. He visited the restaurant at the same time on the same day every week, like clockwork. Gordon always seated him at the same table: right at the front of the dining room, next to the big window overlooking the busy Toronto street beyond.

One day, Gordon was wrestling with paperwork in the back office (the bane of small businesspeople everywhere), so a waiter seated Sam after he arrived. When Gordon finally entered the dining room, Sam greeted him pleasantly. Gordon noted he wore his usual shirt and tie, but had a bright red tartan kilt, an unusual combination.

Gordon traveled down the long narrow restaurant, welcoming other diners who had arrived in his absence, and entered the kitchen area, where he found Amy and the wait staff having a good laugh.

"What's so funny?" he asked.

"It's Sam," said a waiter. "Didn't you notice?"

Gordon looked at him, perplexed.

"He's not wearing any pants!" he blurted out.

Aghast, Gordon realized the "kilt" was a pair of gaudy boxer shorts. Worse: Sam was seated at his usual table, right in front of the window! He hurried back through the dining room and spoke with Sam, gently addressing the fact that he was missing a key item of clothing.

"Yes, of course," Sam replied. "I left my pants at the cleaners across the street. They'll be ready in one hour, when I've finished my lunch."

Gordon saw that, as long as he stayed seated, Sam's lower half was hidden from pedestrians outside by the waist-high wainscoting below the picture window. So as not to shock the diners inside, Gordon made sure Sam's large linen napkin was entirely unfolded in his lap.

Sam enjoyed a wonderful lunch, another tribute to Amy's outstanding culinary skills. (Though he did remark that Gordon seemed quite tense that day. Perhaps he should switch to de-caf? Gordon just smiled a painful smile.)

Sam paid his bill and left, oblivious to the stares of the other diners.

Gordon watched him saunter across the street, as if it was the most natural thing in the world to stroll across a busy Toronto street at midday wearing boxer shorts, and enter the dry cleaners without incident. Several minutes later, Sam emerged, wearing a pair of crisp pressed slacks, and proceeded on his way.

Sam continued to patronize their restaurant, until they sold it to relocate here, and was fully clothed each time. However, whenever he entered, a nervous Gordon always glanced downwards.

***(I once entered a restaurant wearing a fur loincloth and carrying a sword, but that's another story.)***

# MEETINGS ETIQUETTE SORELY LACKING

*Drastic remedies for bozos who disrupt meetings*

As a humble service to people who, whether by choice or coercion, must attend meetings, this article will provide a light-hearted look at what goes wrong and how to fix it.

In my 28-year career of wrangling non-profit associations, I've learned that the many details that go into planning a major meeting, and overcoming the inevitable stressful "Murphy's hiccups", are only half the battle.

The other half is what happens during the meeting itself. I'm not talking about Group Dynamics, Consensus Building, or Tantric Sex. I'm talking about SPI:

Single Person Inconsideration.

For example: the Chair starts the meeting on time, and proceeds smoothly down the agenda, only to have Ms. Always-Late show up and interrupt with loud profuse apologies. Adding insult to agenda, the Chair then feels it necessary to stop the meeting to give Ms. Always-Late a detailed recap of what has happened so far.

That's so unfair to the rest of the group. Dammit, just carry on and let her play catch-up. If she protests, shoot her. You know you want to. Besides, it's perfectly legal in some provinces and all three territories.

Equally galling are those Chairs who won't start a meeting "until everyone's here". What a nice reward to those already present, who took the effort to arrive on time, perhaps despite bad weather or travelling great distances.

Next meeting, the entire group should express its appreciation to the Chair by showing up late - or maybe not at all.

It is a legal requirement that information on major items

needing a vote must be sent to corporate directors ahead of time. Most meeting planners do a great job preparing and sending Briefing Kits in advance; it's essential to smooth-running meetings. So what do you do with the twit who, as the Chair treks along the agenda, makes it very obvious that he hasn't read a single word in the Kit? Worse, Mr. Never-Reads cheerfully admits it to the group.

How does that make the others feel, who took the time to read the Kit? To say nothing of the harried executive who worked late to rush it out? Yet, most times, the Chair makes no rebuke and the rest of the group just shrugs. That's letting the slacker off way too easy. That director is sorely remiss in his due diligence.

We should bring back the death penalty. Some crimes just cry out for it. Especially if it's the Chair who hasn't read the Kit.

People at meetings should work as a team. Productive input and constructive criticism. Makes for a better meeting and helps everyone get out on time. However, some folks feel they're doing the group a favour by being contrary on every decision, just for the sake of being contrary. They feel this "stimulates debate." They speak with an unholy fervor, believing they've been anointed as Devil's Advocate.

They've obviously forgotten what happened to devil worshipers in Salem 400 years ago.

Even worse are those zealots who are Robert's Advocate. Rules of Order, that is. We've all seen meetings bogged down for 20-30 minutes on a minor procedural point that, in the Great Scheme of Things, is worth less than a Planner's Prayer.

These procedural fanatics have missed the whole point of Robert's: the Rules are there to facilitate a meeting, not hamper it. Common sense should prevail. Or a slap upside the head.

Meetings coaches admonish groups not to engage in "side meetings" (one-on-one discussions), especially when someone else has the floor. Some SPIs do it anyway. Often in *sotto voce* that is almost as loud as regular conversation. Most annoying.

Meeting rooms should be rigged with Cones of Silence, like that used in the 1960s TV comedy *Get Smart*. When a disruptive side conversation starts, the Cone immediately lowers over the two offenders. And stays there for the rest of the meeting.

However, what if it's the Chair who engages in side conversations? That sets a fine example. Well, Cone them too. Some meetings would proceed more efficiently if the Chair was silenced for the duration.

The ultimate in rude side conversations occurs when I'm So Much More Important Than The Rest Of You (there's at least one in every group) deliberately sits next to a special guest, like a Cabinet Minister or CEO of a multinational corporation, and proceeds to monopolize him/her in lengthy whispered discourse during the meeting.

We need a return of the Spanish Inquisition for jerks like that, especially because: "*Nobody* expects the Spanish Inquisition!"

Another important etiquette rule in modern meetings should be: "no berry picking while meeting in progress". That means Blackberry, Boysenberry, or Blueberry.

Today, at least one participant in every meeting is always tap-tap-tapping away on an accursed PDA (Personal Digital Assistant). Whatever message they're sending electronically, they're sending the stronger message to the group that their precious fruity device is more important than what's being discussed.

Their fruit needs watering. In the nearest water jug.

(I realize we should pity these Berry-addicts. They've allowed that infernal machine to so dominate their lives that they feel they must even use it at home, nights and weekends, and on vacation. Unfortunately, there is no government-sponsored treatment program to wean them off this addiction. We treat heroin addicts more humanely. It's quite sad.)

The worse SPI of all are those people who are so lonely, so starved for social interaction, that they have no recourse but to call meetings without a valid reason. Whether it lasts half an hour, or half a day, these meetings are a complete waste of time for everyone shanghaied into them, except the desolate soul who needed companionship.

The only cure is for everyone to chip in and buy this person a pet. I hear there's great deals on Boa Constrictors. Encourage cuddling.

*(I'm always ruled out of order at meetings.)*

# THE CEX SHOW

*Clear communication vital to continued survival*

Before relocating to Peterborough 23 years ago, to captain the non-profit association of 1,000 Ontario innkeepers, I worked for the national association of plumbing and heating manufacturers in Toronto. That association owned a huge trade show called the Canadian Environmental Exposition. Its acronym was CEX. (Yes, it was pronounced "sex".)

It was a memorable day when I bounded into the kitchen of our modest condo to inform my wife that I'd just been promoted to co-ordinator of our association's booth display at the show.

"Honey, I'm now in charge of all our CEX arrangements," I announced proudly.

She shot me a strange look. "Oh really? And what exactly does that mean?" She had a large knife in her hand, having just dismembered some vegetables.

"Well, it means everything that happens during CEX," I replied, eyeing the knife which, since my wife had turned to face me, was now pointed right at me. "The set-up, then everything that goes on during the show until the big climax at the end."

"So it's some kind of show now, is it?" she asked, her Irish-green eyes flashing.

"Yeah, it always has been. But now that I'm in charge, it'll be more glitzy, more dynamic than ever. You know I have a theatrical flair."

"Oh, you're a clown, all right. But calling it a show ..."

"What else would you call CEX?" I demanded, a little irritated, because she hadn't yet congratulated me on my promotion. "I mean, you arrange just the right setting, you put your wares on display, then you work hard to please the viewers."

"EXCUSE ME? VIEWERS? Have you been taking pictures

to show people?"

"Of course! I mean, if you ask people to pay money to see CEX, you have to show them some enticing photos beforehand, to lure them in to see the show. It's basic Marketing 101, as you well know, since we took the same university marketing course together." I failed to notice how red her face had turned. My full attention was on the knife, which jabbed the air uncomfortably close to me as she retorted:

"What ... what does marketing have to do with ... with sex?"

"Are you kidding? CEX always needs marketing! If you don't flaunt what you've got to prospective customers, then CEX simply doesn't happen!"

"I. See." Her icy tone would freeze the smile of a politician seeking reelection. Oblivious, I pressed on:

"Anyway, I've some ideas to really liven up our CEX, so it'll be unforgettable for everyone who sees it. We'll use special coloured lights, some dramatic music, and one or two alluring women to model a few products."

"Alluring women!? Is this some kind of weird kinky fantasy? And just what kind of products?"

"Oh, mostly shower stuff, because it's so arousing to see. Just imagine one of those new multi-function showerheads sending a caressing spray cascading down a lithe female body, then switching to a throbbing pulsing stream which - "

"You've completely lost your mind!" she yelled. "I'll have no part of that!"

"Well, I knew you wouldn't," I said. "That's why I'm hiring those models."

With a cry of rage, she slammed the knife down and stormed out of the kitchen. Almost an hour later, my keen whipsmart mind deduced we'd been talking about two completely different things. After I explained the mix-up, she accepted my profuse apologies and even graciously offered to help.

You should have seen my elderly mother-in-law's reaction when she learned we were both involved in putting on a public CEX show.

*(I'm very fortunate I'm still happily married.)*

# PETERBOROUGH AFTER DARK

### *People change when the sun goes down*

A completely-different Peterborough exists after dark, as my son discovered working the night shift, solo, at a local gas station, during his senior year in high school many summers ago. This is his report:

People *change* when the sun retires.

Respectable women, stopping for gas as they head home from work, are transformed hours later when they return to buy smokes, chewing gum and (gasp!) condoms en route to a night of clubbing: their conservative work outfits have been replaced by clingy, revealing clothing.

Similarly, guys morph from Boring Normal to Cool Stud.

These same people often return a third time, in the wee hours, well-lubricated, craving snacks and more cigarettes.

People's conveyances transform after dark too. A big burly man pulls up, squeezed into a compact car that was old when the Beatles were young. After gassing up, the rattletrap wheezes off trailing its own blue smoke screen. Thirty minutes later, the man returns, astride a massive gleaming Harley heralded by its powerful throaty rumble.

He explains the ancient hulk is his "going to work car"; the Harley is his "pleasure machine".

Our hard-working police could save themselves lots of trouble simply by checking with the night gas station attendant about where that evening's illegal field party is being held. The attendant finds out by talking with car loads of teens stopping for fuel and supplies. Ever helpful, he even gives directions to straggling party hounds, who've missed the main convoy.

This will be shocking news to those who believe Peterborough is Ontario's capital of wholesomeness: a thriving escort business exists in our fair city.

The same white land yacht pulls up at the gas station every night at about the same time, with various barely-dressed women jumping out to buy gum or smokes. The driver of the car comes into the store sometimes, paying with bills peeled from one of two huge wads held together by straining money clips.

The night shift provides a variety of entertainment. Like the lady who wobbles into the store at 2 am asking to have air put into her right front tire. My son discovers a tire that is not only flat, but has unconditionally surrendered: it has a huge hole and is off the rim! He finally convinces her it needs replacing. Since he is forbidden to change tires, she starts to do it herself, heedless of her fancy party clothes.

Meanwhile, my son quietly calls 911 and reports a drunk driver. When the police arrive, they discover a besotted damsel whose plates are registered to a different car.

Another evening, long after midnight, two guys try to break into the video store across the street by jimmying the well-lit front door. Of course, alarms sound. Before the police arrive, the would-be thieves scramble up an access ladder onto the roof. Where they might have escaped capture, except their curiosity overcomes them and they peer over the edge to see what the cops are doing....

My son watches the whole thing, calmly sipping coffee; his own private episode of that *Cops* reality show on TV.

His long nights are livened up by an insomniac retired long-distance trucker, who regularly drops by to regale him with tales of the open road, hazardous cargos, incompetent receiving clerks, and seeing Bigfoot on the U.S. west coast. Twice.

A storehouse of conspiracy theories, the *X-Files* show could have used this guy as a resource. ("Did you know that's NOT the *Titanic* down there? It's her sister ship, the *Olympia*. They changed the name plates on her bow.")

Kinda makes the daylight hours seem dull, doesn't it?

**(Every time I go out after dark, I get lost.)**

# TRAFFICKING

## Life in the slow lane

Whenever I must trek to Toronto for meetings, I can't wait until I'm back home in Peterborough, that place of sparkling waters, wonderful scenery, and perpetual zoning appeals to the Ontario Municipal Board. Ah, but getting there! Those fortunate enough to live and work in this beautiful area don't realize the stress of the Kawartha Kommute to and from the Imperious Center Of Canada's Universe, 140 km away.

Here's a typical drive home. (This is an interactive story: travellers from other areas can substitute their own city for Toronto, and their own frequently-jammed highway for the one noted below.) Paragraphs in italics are the words of a traffic helicopter reporter on a Toronto radio station.

*"The Don Valley Parkway northbound is moving well."*

Great! I can get out of downtown TO and up the DVP before it gets clogged. But upon entering the Parkway, I discover traffic moving at the same pace it's taking to replace the ancient Sea King helicopters still used by Canada's military (it's been decades: a new definition of slow).

*"Just flew over the Don Valley again and it still looks good."*

Not! Traffic is a snail's pace of stop-and-starts. A guy on a motorcycle zooms by, travelling between rows of cars. He's in business attire; his tie, flapping jauntily over his shoulder, gives the raspberry to us crawling motorists. Jerk.

*"The DVP northbound is now jammed solid. There's an accident in the right lane near the 401 exit, and everyone is slowing to have a look."*

Wonderful. Another traffic jam caused by the Ghoul Effect: people gawking at mangled metal, *tsk-tsking*, hoping to see blood. A cyclist, who shouldn't even be on this highway, zips by on the shoulder, laughing. Moron.

I've moved ten feet in the last 20 minutes. At least I was smart enough to bring some bottled water. I take a long swig, trying to keep calm.

*"To those caught on the Don Valley, forget the alternate route: there's a Bald Househusband's Pride parade there. Man, the reflection off those chrome domes is blinding!"*

I've inched forward another short distance. At this rate, I'll reach the 401 by the weekend, three days from now. Birds fly by overhead, joyously free. I wish for a shotgun.

*"The police are now at the scene of that accident, and they're getting traffic moving."*

That announcement was thirty minutes ago. Haven't moved a foot. Finished off the water bottle. Getting tired of hearing the same news repeated over and over and over on the radio, but keep the station on to hear the traffic reports. Two kids amble by, making excellent time, thumbing their noses at us. Delinquents.

*"The DVP is still jammed. A section near Eglinton has been cordoned off and turned into a used car lot. There's some great deals down there, folks!"*

I realize it was a big mistake downing that bottle of water. Bathrooms are scarce in the middle of a traffic jam. An old man in a motorized wheelchair rolls along the shoulder. I wonder if he'd swap his wheels for mine, and if the chair's battery would last to Peterborough.

*"BWAH-HA-HA-HA! You poor unfortunate souls!"*

My need for a bathroom has entered the realm of torture. I eye that empty water bottle.

*"Hey folks, I'll set this chopper down and pick up anyone who'll pay $200 cash. Just wave."*

I don't even bother checking my wallet; I run a non-profit association for a living. Suddenly, traffic starts moving. My auto's mobile. Fresh air sweeps in and I realize I was hallucinating from carbon monoxide fumes from all the idling cars. Glad that's over!

*"A herd of escaped cattle has just closed the 401. Those cows aren't mad, but the backed-up motorists sure are! Oh, I've room for one more passenger ..."*

**(I now participate in TO meetings via conference calls.)**

# Chapter Five

## Holidays & Special Occasions

# THE TRUE MEANING
# OF CHRISTMAS
# (CAROLS)

*What olde tyme lyrics mean today*

The talented folks who, years ago, wrote the popular Christmas carols filling the air each holiday season, would be amazed by what some of their lyrics mean today.

For example: *Rudolph the Red-Nosed Reindeer.* Obviously, Rudolph has a serious drinking problem; that explains his crimson schnozz. Yet instead of enrolling the poor creature in the North Pole chapter of Alcoholics Anonymous, Santa exploits Rudolph's disability by placing him at the head of his team every Christmas Eve. Rather than encouraging Rudolph to follow the 12-step program, Santa buys him drinks at the Iceberg Bar, so the critter's nose is bright when the Jolly Old Elf needs it most. Santa's flouting drinking-and-driving laws, too. It's quite a sad song, really.

What about the carol: *God Rest Ye Merry, Gentlemen?* It's fine for gentlemen to rest, but what about the gentlewomen? Women deserve it far more, because they're so busy around Christmas. Look at all the cooking, cleaning, wrapping and decorating they do. I get exhausted just watching them. That song needs a major rewrite.

There's serious privacy issues in *Santa Claus Is Comin' To Town.* Pere Noel makes Peeping Toms seem harmless. He's had his elves secretly install state-of-the-art surveillance gear in our homes. Look at the evidence: "he knows when you are sleeping, he knows when you're awake, he knows if you've been bad or good." Talk about intrusive! We have a national Protection of Privacy law nowadays. Why aren't the RCMP after this guy?

An increasing disrespect for authority infects our society, and no wonder. A beloved Christmas carol encourages this: *Frosty The*

*Snowman*. Listen to the lyrics. Promising some wild fun, the snowy desperado of no fixed address leads an unruly gang of kids down the streets of town, right to the traffic cop, but only pauses a moment when the officer hollers "Stop!". See? Teaching impressionable youth civil disobedience. Shameful.

*Let It Snow!* is about an unmarried couple up to hanky-panky. "The lights are turned way down low", and they're in front of a romantic crackling fire. Canoodling, for sure. But that's not the issue; we assume they're consenting adults. No, the issue is that she callously shoves him out into a raging blizzard afterwards. "The weather outside is frightful", says the song. We never learn if the poor guy makes it home safely.

His girlfriend probably wanted him gone before Santa came down her chimney - a futile effort, since Surveillance Santa already knows she's been quite naughty.

The presents delivered during *The Twelve Days Of Christmas* were sent by a vindictive ex-lover. Think about the mess made by a partridge, two turtle doves, three french hens, four calling birds, six geese, seven swans, and the eight cows those maids were a-milking. The hapless recipient has to clean that up. Pawning those five gold rings would just about pay the hefty fine for the Health Code violations.

And what about the cacophony of nine drummers drumming, 10 pipers piping, and 11 formerly-dancing ladies now running shrieking from the amorous advances of 12 leaping lords? Result: noise disturbance complaints filed by angry neighbours.

After *Grandma Got Run Over By A Reindeer*, the family sued Santa for reckless driving (a drunken reindeer led his team, after all), causing severe emotional trauma (on Christmas Eve!). The court awarded them millions. Santa was jailed and Rudolph was ordered into rehab.

Merry Christmas!

*(I do hope my stocking isn't crammed with coal this Christmas.)*

# MORE TRUE MEANINGS OF CHRISTMAS (CAROLS)

*Modern interpretations of other olde lyrics*

The previous story discussed how the lyrics of some beloved Christmas carols have very different meanings today; meanings the songwriters never envisioned when they crafted them years ago. At the risk of a permanent spot on Santa's naughty list, here are more interpretations of other holiday carols:

The activity in *Jingle Bells* is actually quite dangerous. "Dashing through the snow in a one horse open sleigh". C'mon, how sane is it to ride around in a convertible, with the top down, in our sub-zero Canadian winter? It places an irresponsible strain on our beleaguered health care system, as sleigh-riders come down with nasty colds, pneumonia, bronchitis, frostbite and lips frozen onto their seat-mate's lips.

Park that convertible in the barn, buddy, and take public transit. Bonus: buses don't befoul the *Winter Wonderland* with horse poop. Let's keep Christmas white!

Nowadays, *Ring Christmas Bells* refers to cash register bells, because the holiday season is more commercialized than ever. Canada's Gross Domestic Product is heavily dependant upon strong Christmas retail sales. So it's our patriotic duty to ring those bells vigorously.

In fact, those bells shouldn't even be called "Christmas", since they ring longest after December 25, during the modern sales frenzy known as Boxing Week (which started out as a single day when all the stores were closed).

*It's Beginning to Look a Lot Like Christmas* should now more properly be sung in September, when Christmas items start appearing in stores. Singing it around Christmas is inappropriate for another reason: the stores are cleaned out of all the good stuff by then.

When Bing Crosby croons *White Christmas*, he's not alone in dreaming of a Yuletide smothered in snow. Legions of skiers, snowmobilers, ATVers, tobogganers, snowmen makers, snowball fighters and one horse open sleighers are fervently hoping for it too.

So are harried women, desperate to get the kids, including the big one they married, out of the house for several hours during the holidays, so they can get a little peace and quiet. It's not for nothing that the murder rate soars this time of year.

The journey of *We Three Kings of Orient Are* would be extremely difficult nowadays, what with passport requirements, increased border security, x-rays, baggage searches, body pats, and the lengthy quarantine of foreign camels. To easily deliver those gifts today, the royal threesome would have to ship them by UPS. Even then, Mary and Joseph would be saddled with hefty customs duties.

And the gifts would arrive after Christmas anyway, since customs agents don't work over the holidays.

Today, these lyrics in *Deck the Halls* can cause confusion: "Don we now our gay apparel." Modern science has proven that it's not the clothes one wears that makes one gay. In fact, folks can be happy no matter what they wear.

*Silent Night* may have been accurate when the carol debuted in 1818, but not today. Christmas is anything but silent, what with the cacophony of joyful noise that erupts: people caroling, parties hosting, friends toasting, children laughing, reindeer prancing, sleigh bells jingling, church bells ringing, angels on high singing, drummer boys pa rum pum pum pumming, frosty snowmen thumpetty thumping, and everybody *Joy to the World*ing.

Sheesh, what a racket!

Bah, humbug!

*(I just know my jumbo-size Christmas stocking will forever remain empty.)*

# HOW THE GOVERNMENT STOLE CHRISTMAS

*Bureaucratic Grinches take over*

As federal, provincial and municipal governments intrude more and more into our lives, with legislation, regulation and consternation, it's only a matter of time until bureaucrats end up running Christmas.

It will start with Santa's Workshop.

Santa, overextended financially after years of giving away free toys, would finally have his many loans called in by Canadian banks reeling from bad loans to the American subprime mortgage market. The jolly old elf would have to declare bankruptcy.

China, coveting the alleged oil reserves under the North Pole, would purchase the property. Our federal government, hounded by criticism that it allowed yet another Canadian icon to be sold to foreigners, would buy it back for billions more than the Chinese paid.

Under federal ownership, Santa would lose his decision-making authority, because all major decisions go through the Prime Minister's office, to ensure total control.

Frustrated at being a mere figurehead, Santa would abandon his centuries-old responsibilities and escape to some tropical island with the Missus, a fat government pension indexed for inflation, and fur-trimmed swimsuits.

A new federal department would promptly be created (HoHoCanada), with a multi-billion dollar budget and staffed by the hundreds of bureaucrats deposed when the Gun Registry finally ended.

With career bureaucrats in charge, Santa's Workshop would be a very different place.

First, everything would become Politically Correct. Elves

would henceforth be called Unique Workers, because "elves" implies vertically-challenged persons who could be open to ridicule, and we can't have that.

The workforce would quickly be unionized, under CUPE (Canadian Union of Pointy Ears).

Affirmative Action would be implemented, requiring the hiring of visible minorities like Newfoundlanders, farmers, honest lawyers and English-speaking Canadians. Women too.

Toy production would plummet, because of the many mandatory hours spent learning both North Pole languages (Inuit and Beluga).

Countless additional hours would be consumed to meet government labour requirements for training in Health and Safety, Care and Feeding of Reindeer (immediately followed by Hazardous Materials Handling), Customer Service for Civil Servants (say that with a straight face), and Sensitivity to Persons with Disabilities (like parents unable to follow "simple" toy assembly instructions written by drunken MIT engineers).

Official Toy Requisition Procedures would be instituted. No more phonetically-misspelled yet teacher-approved letters to Santa crayoned on paper. Instead, thick forms jammed with tiny print would have to be completed, in triplicate. One form for each requested toy would be the rule, causing massive clear-cutting of our precious remaining forests to make enough forms.

Toy requests would be handled with the same speed and efficiency as equipment requests made by our Canadian Armed Forces; the child would be an adult, with children of his/her own, before the toy arrived.

The toys themselves would have to reflect Canada's vast ethnic diversity, with instructions printed in so many languages that it would be impossible to find the official French and English wording.

Any toy with even the remotest potential to be harmful to children, would be discontinued. So classic playthings like Slinky, Lego, Nerf balls, Play Doh and Easy Bake Ovens would become collector's items.

Santa's famous reindeer team would be retired, because it would not be environmentally-conscious to have poop factories overfly urban areas. Instead, presents would be delivered by Expresspost, meaning they would arrive after Christmas, broken after being crammed into mail boxes regardless of "Fragile" stickers.

Well, I say the heck with Political Correctness! I say: "Merry Christmas!"

*(Along with retail staff, by December 24, I am saturated with Christmas music that started playing in stores the day after Hallowe'en slunk back to its crypt.)*

# O CHRISTMAS TREE

*A snow-bound family outing*

Years ago, when our son was five, we decided our family Christmas experience should include the personal harvesting of a live Christmas tree.

We soon learned that our normally-gracious neighbours didn't take kindly to us cutting down the spruces in their yards (did you know that dog bites really hurt?).

So we patronized a local tree farm, welcoming a trek into winter's wonderland to enhance the experience.

Our first time was quite memorable. Wearing full winter gear, we brought a saw, toboggan to haul out the freshly-cut tree, thermos of hot cocoa, compass, waterproof matches, freeze-dried trail rations, emergency "foil" blanket, flare, survival handbook and a satellite phone. Just in case.

The tree farm was a veritable forest, thick with trees from small to giant. However, said forest was located some distance from the parking lot. No worries. We had come for a trek.

We installed our excited son aboard the toboggan and, with Dad The Donkey pulling, off we went.

With much huffing and puffing on mom and dad's part, due to the deep snow, and cries of encouragement from the freeloader, we finally reached the woods.

It was a Currier & Ives scene: row upon row of aromatic evergreens, artfully decorated with fresh-fallen snow, which sparkled in the crisp air.

After much deliberation and careful inspection of what seemed like every spruce in the forest, the perfect tree was selected. My wife got out the camera, while I dropped to my knees in the white stuff at the base of the tree and began sawing.

I forgot about the white stuff on the tree above me.

As I cut the trunk, the spruce expressed its anger at being kidnaped from its favorite spot by dumping its snowy coat on me. To be specific, upon my head and down the gap between coat collar and neck.

As the cold wet mass engulfed me, my wife and son exploded into gales of laughter. I exploded into a few unChristmaslike phrases.

The more I sawed, the more snow landed on me. My son was turning red from laughing so hard. I was turning red for another reason.

Finally, its snowy bombs exhausted and its revenge complete, the tree fell.

We swapped Laughing Boy for Christmas Tree on the toboggan, shared the contents of the thermos, then started back.

To a small boy with snow up to his hips, the return trek was arduous. It soon became apparent he'd never make it out of the forest, much less back to the car. Motivating him with tales of what wolves did to tasty youngsters proved fruitless; little legs and deep snow simply didn't work.

While I agonized over what to abandon, tyke or tree, my wife announced a practical solution: the tree stayed on the toboggan, which she would pull, and I would carry our offspring atop my shoulders.

The kid's added weight served to push me deeper into the snow as I slogged onwards.

His cheerful reminders of how funny I'd looked with avalanches cascading upon me didn't help.

Eventually, we made it back to the warm, dry car. My wife and I were exhausted and I was quite chilled, courtesy of my soaked back. I could almost feel the first sniffles starting.

But on the drive home, our son's bright eyes and animated conversation meant it had all been worth it.

Then he announced he planned to bring the photos into class for Show and Tell.

And he couldn't wait to do it all again next year.

*(Live Christmas trees should come pre-cut, snow-free, fully decorated and delivered to one's door.)*

# REINDEER CALLING CARDS

*The perils of over-decorating*

Be careful about how elaborate your Christmas decorations are, or this could happen to you.

We were dining with two friends (Thomas and Geraldine) at one of Peterborough's intimate fine restaurants, when the chef emerged to inquire about our meals. After expressing our full-bellied delight, we complimented her on her Christmas decorations. The conversation evolved to discuss how wonderful some of the outdoor decorations were around our fair city. The chef said an ideal flourish to an outdoor display was the addition of "reindeer droppings": homemade chocolate truffles with grated carrots mixed in. Would look very authentic, she assured us, if they mysteriously appeared Christmas morn when young kids, wide-eyed with the wonder of Santa, looked out the window.

While my wife and I felt truffles belonged in one's stomach, not on one's lawn, Tom and Gerry, who had three youngsters, thought it was a wonderful idea.

The following week, the carefully-prepared "reindeer droppings" debuted at their family Christmas Circus. ("Circus" because they had Tom's brother and wife as guests, with their own three urchins.) On Christmas Eve, just before he went to bed, Tom snuck outside and artfully scattered truffle/carrot lumps on the snow of his front lawn, near the living room picture window.

Next morning, bright-eyed kids rousted bleary-eyed parents out of bed, Merry Christmas was loudly proclaimed, presents were opened, hugs and thank yous were given, and good cheer filled the crowded living room. Then, after several not-too-subtle hints, the youngsters looked outside and were awed by the surprise display of fresh reindeer poop. Undeniable proof that Saint Nick really existed (or that our local Riverview Zoo had suffered another break-out; this time of reindeer). Luckily, it had not snowed during the night, so the "droppings" were quite noticeable. The chef had been right: the things certainly looked authentic.

Later, over breakfast, the secret came out that the "droppings" were really chocolate truffles with carrot shavings. The kids were shocked. Not at the deception, but that mostly-sane adults would waste something as precious as chocolate. After breakfast, while the parents sat around with their coffee and debated how to entertain their brood for the day, the four oldest urchins quietly shrugged on their coats and slipped outside.

About ten minutes later, Gerry announced she would recreate the "reindeer droppings" for dessert that evening.

"Ha! I wonder if the kids will eat them," laughed Tom.

"Sure!" boomed a youngster as the outdoor foursome trooped into the kitchen, cheeks rosy and knees dusty with snow. "They taste just great!"

"How do you know?" asked Gerry.

The rapscallions grinned triumphantly. One announced:

"Well, we thought it was, like, a majorly shame to let awesome, like, chocolate truffly things go to waste, so we, like, just snuck outside and ate 'em!"

"You ... you ate them all?" exclaimed Tom.

"Yeppir! All 15 of 'em! We counted! They were, like, really cold an' hard, but they sure were, like, good!"

Beaming like they just learned school had been canceled until Easter, the scavengers decamped for the rec room and the video games therein. Tom looked at Gerry and said:

"Um, I think I only put out 14 truffles last night."

"That's true, I only made 14," affirmed Gerry.

The four adults, faces looking a little green, stared open-mouthed at each other.

"Let's, um, let's just keep this to ourselves," suggested Gerry, swallowing hard. The others nodded.

Forrest Gump's famous saying is especially apt in this instance: "Life is like a box of chocolates: you never know what you're going to get."

*(I learned early never to eat yellow snow either.)*

# CRACKING THE CHRISTMAS CODE

*What merchandise and retailer messages really mean*

'Tis the season to be jolly - so force a smile as you hand over your plastic to pay for yet another gift on your seemingly-endless list. But beware: Christmas comes with its own code, which everyone braving the holiday hordes should understand. As a public service, I shall translate:

*"Easy to install"* on packages of computer and video stuff only applies to those under the age of 25. They'll hook it up in half the time, without reading the instructions.

*"Some assembly required"* means you're doomed; no amount of instructions can help. You'll be missing key parts, too.

*"Suitable for all ages"* means except teenagers. Just give money.

*"One size fits all"* is quite true, but only if you're that family in Moose Jaw on whom our national sizing standards are based. Otherwise, forget it. Give gift certificates instead.

*"Our lowest prices ever"* means only until Boxing Week sales, whereupon prices plummet to levels that make pre-Christmas shoppers weep. Again, give gift certificates.

*"The latest style"* fools parents and other hopelessly out-of-touch adults. It was the latest style all right - last year. As your kids will tell you Christmas morning.

*"Open 'til midnight for your last-minute shopping"* means if you once again foolishly left your Christmas shopping until the eleventh hour (yes, guys, I'm talking to you), then shopkeepers will kindly stay open late so you may purchase the leftover stuff that nobody else wanted.

*"Fun for the whole family"* on board games is a highly optimistic claim. The only time your whole family will play together is during power failures when computers and home

entertainment centres sit cold and lifeless. Board game manufacturers should be honest and include candles.

*"Satisfaction guaranteed"* applies to the merchants, who are very satisfied when you depart clutching your treasures. The guarantee only applies to you after enduring torturously-long line-ups after Christmas to return the goods.

*"Items returned must be in original packaging"* is non-negotiable. So on Christmas morn, don't let Johnny destroy the packaging in his eagerness to get at the stuff within. Husbands should show some restraint in front of the kids.

*"A great selection"* was true - in September. The selection was gone before Hallowe'en. What's left are in sizes and colours only suitable for less than 5% of the population. None of whom are in your family.

*"The woman in your life will love it"* does not refer to power tools, sports equipment, or automotive accessories. Sorry guys. It applies to gifts that cause your Significant Other to heroically thank you for what the salesperson assured you would be a wonderful present and what she knows is going right back to the store. Especially lingerie that even anorexic super-models couldn't wear without immediately falling out of.

*"Buy now for Christmas delivery"* is a cruel practical joke. Says so in the small print.

*"Attractively gift-boxed"* means the recipient will know you were too lazy to wrap it yourself.

*"Pre-Christmas sale"* means the retailer is having cash flow problems and may not be around after Christmas to accept returns.

Yes, there's lots more to the holiday season than presents. There's family 'n' friends, turkey 'n' stuffing, religious celebrations, helping the needy, carols, snow, hangovers. But you must also survive the stores. It's character-building.

And doing your shopping on the Internet is cheating.

Me? I do all my Christmas shopping at 11 pm December 24. What's so wrong about giving McCertificates?

**(I learned all this the hard way.)**

# NEW YEAR'S UNRESOLUTIONS

*Undaunted, unimproved, unrepentant - so there!*

January is a depressing month. Family and friends have gone home after the holidays and Christmas bills arrive daily even if we glue the mailbox shut.

Plus: every year we add to our misery by making New Year's Resolutions; the most depressing thing of all. We know it's just a matter of time before we break them.

So let's break this awful cycle instead! As a public service, inspired by the Unbirthday Song in Disney's classic *Alice in Wonderland*, I hereby present these Unresolutions:

**The Diet Unresolution:** "I solemnly swear that, because diets are a pain, making me and everyone around me feel miserable, and because no normal person can stay on them for long, and especially because salads are indeed meant only for rabbits, therefore I shall no longer diet. I am happier eating what I want, when I want. If I'm chubbier than I should be, I will remember that is only according to medical opinions from disgruntled thin people who can't stand happy chubby folks. Life is too short for diets.

"Besides, the restaurants in town deserve my patronage; they have employees to support. Therefore, I will practice good citizenship through eating, preferably with wine."

**The Exercise Unresolution:** "I solemnly swear that I shall not exercise in the New Year, because exercise is dull in its repetitiveness, overly-sweaty, and often painful, especially when your personal trainer wallops you for not trying harder. It is a cruelty invented by a secret cabal of phys ed teachers frustrated that they never won Olympic gold in their youth, pharmaceutical companies eager to sell pain-killers, and chiropractors.

"Exercise machines are the modern descendants of medieval torture devices, and have the same result: crippling and eventually killing you. If I can bend down to pick up my TV remote without shortness of breath, then I'm in good enough shape."

**The Beauty Unresolution:** "I solemnly swear that I shall not go under a surgeon's knife for any cosmetic reason whatsoever. I shall be happy with what God and my parents' genes gave me, walking proud in my uniqueness. If others find me less than appealing, if small children laugh at me, then I shall pity them, for they know not that inside I am a radiant being.

"I shall also not spend half my paycheque on beauty creams, lotions, face-paint and notions, for while such expensive products may disguise my outer faults, it is a temporary and untrue camouflage, resulting in often-fatal shock to one's partner when they are removed."

(Note: this entire Unresolution can also apply to women.)

**The Niceness Unresolution:** "I solemnly swear that I shall not artificially try to be nicer at work and at home. I am who I am. My personality was set in infancy, after my mother dropped me on my head several times. If people are nice to me, I shall be nice to them. If people are miserable to me, then why on earth should I be nice to them? They'll think I'm insane, or worse, a politician.

"However, I vow to start each day with a happy, cheerful outlook - at least until I have to get out of bed."

**The Family Time Unresolution:** "I will not spend more time with my family until I first ask: do they want to spend more time with me?" (Refer to Niceness Unresolution and be prepared for an answer you may not like.)

There, now don't you feel better already? Here's to a guilt-free New Year's!

***(I unresolve to spend less time at my computer.)***

# LOVE IS A
# MANY-SPLENDORED THING

*We're going to need a bigger card shop*

Around February 14, people's thoughts often turn to love. Yet despite its creation by chocolatiers, florists and greeting card companies to profitably celebrate the love between two people, it occurred to me that, in fairness, other kinds of love also deserve to be saluted during Valentine's Day.

For example, what about the love of fans for their favorite sport? Whether to play it on weekends, all sweaty and courting injury every second (love hurts), or to lustily cheer it from the stands or in front of the TV, lubricated with the finest hops.

That kind of love brings a tear to one's eye. Especially if your team loses.

Strong passion also exists between collectors and their collectibles, be they model trains, vintage planes, classic cars, sports and non-sports cards, comic books, Barbie dolls, old milk bottles, jewelry, art, wine, antiques, celebrity toenail clippings, or outhouses. You name a thing, and someone somewhere is passionate about collecting it. Proof? They cry if their spouse forces them to get rid of it. So that's love too.

Then there's the love of a dog for its master(s), or a cat for itself. Total, unconditional affection. Especially around mealtimes. Speaking of meals, everyone has a favorite dish, the mere mention of which causes them to salivate. That's love right there. And it's not to be taken lightly. It's a very dangerous love; just try standing between people and the all-you-can-eat buffet as it opens.

There's the love - often very expensive - that people have for their homes, or their cars, boats, planes, bicycles, horses, snowmobiles, or ATVs.

There's a whole category of love between some women and

their shoes. All 315 pairs. It's a forbidden love too, as males are forbidden to encourage a culling of the herd lest, afterwards, they are then dragged off to shop for more and forbidden to quit until every shoe in every shoe store in every mall within 100 miles has been tried on. Twice.

And I've only scratched the surface. There's many other loves, such as:

A child's love for a special toy, or stuffed animal, or parent's shoulder.

A teenager's love for the latest rock star, computer game, or ripped jeans.

A man's love for his gourmet kitchen.

A woman's love for her woodworking tools.

A photographer's love for the perfect picture.

A sailor's love for the perfect wind.

A butcher's love for a superb cut of meat.

A golfer's love for a hole-in-one.

An actor's love for a flawless performance.

A mother's love for peace and quiet and long bubble baths.

A father's love for big hugs from his kids.

An author's love (often unrequited) for receiving payment for his/her work.

If all these other types of love were also celebrated on Valentine's Day, just think of the new markets for florists and greeting card creators.

Such as specialized floral arrangements for sports fans (like a real "Rose Bowl" for football enthusiasts). Ladies enamored with their shoes could receive the "petunia pump".

A host of specialty Valentine greeting cards would be in demand for the many different loves that needed commemorating. ("Do you have a card for someone who loves gardening naked?")

In this age of political correctness, the myriad varieties of love deserve equal celebration. Let's broaden our horizons!

(Now please excuse me; I'm off to find a Valentine's card for someone who loves to bay at the moon from his rooftop.)

*(Valentines are also needed for people who love to write wryly humourous stories.)*

# CUPID GO HOME

*If Cupid were around today, he'd be smothered in lawsuits*

As Valentine's Day approaches, naturally my thoughts turn to chocolate ... er, romance. The mythological Roman god of love, Cupid, is lucky his era ended thousands of years ago. He'd be in so much trouble if he existed today.

Today's romantic relationships are much more complicated than in bygone years. Back then, all Cupid had to do was fire his little arrows, the couple would fall into each other's arms, and that would be that. Instant relationship.

Nowadays, folks would be quite upset at being shot with arrows. Besides the physical assault with a deadly weapon, (bad enough in this age of increased street violence), people would be worried about contracting HIV. Does Cupid disinfect his arrows between victims, or does he pluck them out and immediately reuse them? And what about the danger of putting someone's eye out with those things? Didn't his Mama warn him about playing with sharp objects?

Cupid would be slapped with so many lawsuits, his cherubic little head would spin.

And federal government bureaucrats would feel compelled to create a Bow-and-Arrow Registry, upsetting law-abiding recreational archers everywhere and wasting billions more of our taxpayer dollars.

But Cupid would have other problems: the law would take a dim view of a buck-naked winged juvenile flying around. Then there's folks whose morals would be highly offended by the sight of this smiling imp-in-the-buff.

More lawsuits. Maybe some serious jail time (public indecency and flying without a licence).

Besides all that, Cupid would be mystified at the complexities of relationships between young people today. Falling in love is often the last step.

First, there's whether or not each person uses the same email system; it's far more important that text-messaging and blogging be compatible, than the persons themselves.

Second, does the potential couple have harmonious music devices: satellite radios, iPods, and MP3 players (to say nothing of the same tastes in music)?

Third, do they each have the same multi-use phone (Blackberry, Blueberry, or Boysenberry)?

Fourth, can they afford to be an e-couple, each earning sufficient money to pay the massive phone bills that will result from all that text-messaging, voice-messaging, picture-phone transmittals, and - how quaint - actual voice-to-voice communication?

Fifth, do each drive the right kind of car?

If all the above works out, and thoughts turn to co-habiting, can they both agree on what satellite or cable TV system to use? Can they afford two dedicated computer hook-up lines? Does their proposed apartment have enough electrical outlets to recharge two complete sets of multiple electronic devices, all at the same time?

Do they both like the same kind of take-out food? (After all, who has the time or expertise to cook these days?) Can they agree on a maid service to clean their apartment? (No cool cosmopolitan couple actually does - ugh - bathrooms anymore.) And, oh yeah, can they afford the rent?

Finally, after years of co-habiting, then maybe the couple decides to get married. Which not only bedevils Cupid, but the couple's family and friends, who don't know what wedding presents to get a trendy twosome who've been living together for eons.

Yes, Cupid would be completely superfluous today - except on greeting cards. In fact, he could sue for years of unpaid royalties for using his cute likeness on those cards.

The money he'd get might just cover his fines and legal bills from those weapons and indecent exposure convictions.

*(I already suffer from slings and arrows.)*

# PUT-UPON POPS

## *The burdens placed upon fathers*

Reflecting upon my 25-year apprenticeship as a father, I've come to realize a truism:

Fathers are really put-upon.

Yep, as soon as our offspring reach a certain age, and after we dads assume the time-honoured hands-and-knees position, they are put upon our backs, there to be ridden all over the house, to gales of laughter. The price we pay: years of future chiropractic care for a bad back. (Now at our expense - thanks, Ontario Premier Dalton.)

At parades or in crowded malls, junior is put upon our shoulders, there to see better and to imperiously steer the course of The Good Ship Daddy by turning our head in the desired direction. Our price: loss of hair (see Author's photo), as the little rugrat grabs at our topknot to maintain balance.

Even though the male of the species is poorly engineered for the task, both biologically and mechanically, the baby is put upon the table in front of us, there to have its diaper changed. Our price: a strong desire not to have any more kids. And years of therapy.

Watching TV at the end of a long day, or during Sunday afternoon sports games, as we recline on the couch to coach our televised team to victory, the little nipper is put upon our ever-expanding comfortable stomachs, there to fall into a deep and drooly sleep. Our price: the chiropractor again as we strain our neck trying to see the TV around the slumbering body. And a very wet shirt.

At our child's first Christmas, after we dress up as Saint Nick, our pride and joy is put upon our knee, there to receive his/her first present. Our price: a future hearing aid, because the brat shrieks at being put upon this stranger with the huge frightening white beard.

Each year, outlandish hats are put upon our balding heads (see fourth paragraph), as we help our little nose-miners celebrate their birthday, surrounded by hordes of screaming size-challenged barbarians intent on wanton destruction. Our price: same as in paragraph five.

Our teenaged daughter's head is put upon our shoulder, as we comfort the tearful girl after the breakup of her first serious relationship. Our price: having future boyfriends screened by a battery of psychological compatibility tests.

Our newly-licenced teenaged son's hand is put upon our back, as he pats us in gratitude after we agree to his 4,500th plea to borrow the family car. Our price: the family car.

A second mortgage is put upon our house, so that we may send our heirs to an institution of higher learning, there to achieve wonderful grades and an eventual worthwhile career. Our price: cringing every time we learn about our kids' latest wild party or insane daredevil stunt.

With a smile put upon our face by fortitude worthy of Gandhi himself, we graciously receive yet another tie as a present. Our price: wearing it.

And throughout our children's lives, their arms are put upon our upper bodies, as they give us frequent hugs to express their love for us. Our price: a very unmanly lump in the throat. Greatest feeling in the world.

Yes, fathers are put upon this earth to be put-upon. But we wouldn't have it any other way. The rewards are truly priceless.

(For everything else, there's MasterCard.)

*(I realize that mothers are also put-upon, but this story is about dads for once, okay?)*

# FATHER KNOWS LAST

*Why do kids always go to mom first?*

With Father's Day a June tradition, I realized something: children still don't consider fathers as user-friendly as mothers. The proof is that fathers are always the last to know. About everything. Kids still go to their mothers first with important news. Especially the bad news.

This is bothersome. Over the past few decades, we dads have expended considerable effort to become more approachable, more sharing, more nurturing. In short, to become just like moms.

So we deserve a good return on our investment.

Compared to most of our own fathers back in prehistoric times (before colour TV), we dads today do more household chores, spend more time with our kids, and are much more accessible. We're with our cherubs from the exact moment of birth, until the day they announce they've had quite enough of us and leave to strike out on their own (around age 40). In contrast, our fathers never even had the option of Paternity Leave when we brats hatched ourselves.

But all this PC (Paternal Correctness) obviously hasn't worked. Kids today still don't see both parents as equally user-friendly. Examples abound:

In elementary school, when his best buddy dumps him for an even better buddy, who does your frustrated son turn to first for advice? Mom.

In high school, who finds out first if your daughter has found her One True Love, or has just broken up with That Miserable Jerk (often the same boy, only weeks apart)? Mom.

Bad report cards? Schoolyard bullies? Children's gossip? Mom.

Who's the first to know that your (hopefully-married)

daughter is pregnant? Mom.

It just ain't fair. We dads have put in the time, we've made the effort, we've changed our behavior, yet we're still treated like The Bad Guy. Case in point:

A male friend of mine, properly housebroken, was vacuuming one day, when his 10-year-old son sidled in, looking like a civil servant caught misappropriating funds. The boy asked where mom was. My friend said he didn't know, and what was the matter? The urchin said "nothing" (of course). Ignoring the readily-available and completely-receptive parent right in front of him, he promptly embarked upon an expedition to track down The Elusive Mother. Long minutes later, mom came up to dad and revealed that their pride 'n' joy had broken a garage door window playing ball.

See my point? Why did the boy feel it necessary to go to mom first, to have her act as the intermediary between him and dad? My friend was every inch the nurturing, buddy-buddy dad that government legislation now requires. Heck, he was even doing the vacuuming! How mom-like can a guy get?

But no, just like in the 1950s and 60s, his son went to mom first. Then hung back, cautiously, ready to flee at the first sign of an explosion, while mom brokered the bad news.

To his credit, my friend defied the cliche of The Angry Dad. He merely gave his offspring a reproachful look, then went outside to survey the damage. That's when he discovered that all three garage door windows had been smashed.

I'm pleased to report that it was mom who flipped out; not because of the damage, but because junior had only told her one-third of the story.

So, on Father's special Day, I implore kids of all ages to go to dad first with the Important News, especially any Bad News.

Trust me, he'll really appreciate it.

*(Despite decades of model dad behavior, I'm still always the last to know.)*

# WHY ARE FATHERS SO SPECIAL ANYWAY?

*Why dads deserve their day*

Some people question why dads deserve their own special Father's Day.

After all, despite decades of feminist consciousness-raising, it's mothers who still shoulder most of the domestic chores, even if they also work outside the home (sorry guys, putting the toilet seat down doesn't qualify as a domestic chore). So moms definitely deserve their Mother's Day.

However, besides the obvious, Mother's Day would be difficult without dads: that Sunday, many fathers go grocery shopping with their kids, leaving mom at home (hopefully relaxing in bed and not scrubbing bathrooms). Do you realize the stress untrained males go through, shopping for groceries? *(See page 76.)*

And then those nice dads take mom and family out to Mother's Day brunch or dinner, heroically concealing anguish when the bill arrives.

Granted, it's mothers who go through the excruciating pain of giving birth. Us guys can't top that. Ah, but what about fathers' labour pains? Like holding your wife's hand during delivery, gamely encouraging her while your hand is mashed into pulp by her death grip. Or that special pain only fathers know, when your head smacks the hospital floor as you faint after seeing all the blood.

It's moms who, all alone, must deal with hordes of demons, vampires, superheroes, pirates and princesses who invade their home every Hallowe'en. Where're the dads? Out in the haunted cold, dark, windy, sometimes rainy night, ignoring the pain in their feet and the numbness in their ears, shepherding their own little monsters around the neighbourhood - and the next neighbourhood - and the one after that - as their children succumb to an avarice greater than the Canada Revenue Agency.

Sure, moms do most of the cooking (and reap the praise). Who gives a kind thought to dads stuck outside barbequing in all kinds of weather, battling the heat of burners set to max, engulfed in enough thick smoke and flame to justify a three-alarm fire, wringing that last bit of moistness and taste out of those expensive steaks? What about dad's hurt feelings as his entire family, presented with the charred results of his culinary expertise, announces they've just become vegetarians?

Dads, like golfers, play with a handicap: females can show all their feelings, but society insists that males keep their gentler emotions bottled up. So kids often mistake their dads for being aloof, reserved. That adds a special challenge to being a father, like smiling stoically through the school play when your child misses their cue - three times. Or merely wincing as your star athlete plays their little heart out, but just misses that last tie-making goal and their team loses. Because of our handicap, it takes determined effort to offer encouraging words, hugs or tears; we're hard-wired to yell, curse, or hit something with a club. Belch, too.

Sure there's soccer moms. But there's also hockey dads. And baseball dads, fishing dads, chess dads, kite-flying dads, and let's-go-for-ice-cream dads. Ditto cartoon-watching buddies, bedtime story performers, and kamikaze tummy-blowers.

There's no denying that the skills of a mom are legion. Yet dads have skills too, like toy and bicycle assembly and repair, chauffeur, swimming instructor, coach, automobile consultant, clown, resume polisher, Santa, date interrogator, wandering downstairs in their underwear at the wrong time, and, especially, mom's assistant.

The evidence proves that dads are special too. We deserve our own day. In our hairy, bombastic way, we've earned it as much as moms.

Besides, moms said we could.

*(I'm still perfecting my dad skills after 25 years.)*

# MOTEL MACABRE

*Hallowe'en hospitality at its best*

As you shepherd your little monsters around the spooky streets on October 31, be careful you don't step into *The Twilight Zone*, where this place might exist...

A unique inn is falling apart at the end of 1313 Nightmare Lane: the Dead-End Motel. It is owned and operated by Bela and Lucretia Toombes, a charming couple who've been married for 47 years, 34 of which when they were alive. The motel does a thriving business, as Bela explains: "more guests check in, than check out."

Lucretia adds: "one of our most popular packages is dinner with funeral." The package includes an after-dinner cordial called Lucretia's Surprise, followed immediately by an old-fashioned horse-drawn hearse tour of the village, ending with internment at a local cemetery.

All guest rooms feature Eternalrest mattresses, which inspired the motel's slogan: "We promise you'll sleep like the dead."

"Our rooms are never cleaned," says Bela proudly. "All the cobwebs, dust and bugs are authentic. And we don't charge extra for the bugs."

In-room entertainment includes real blood dripping down the walls ("none of that fake canned stuff here," sniffs Lucretia), and mattresses that always get a squeal from guests when they lie down and feel things moving beneath them. The TV plays the Horror Channel 24/7, showing bloodcurdling movies and classic scary episodes of *The Munsters, Addams Family, The Twilight Zone* and Question Period in Parliament.

Pets are welcome ("Chef Igor is always looking for new menu items", smiles Bela), but werewolves must be kept on a chain.

The motel has several theme suites: The Guillotine Room ("You'll lose your head over this one," cackles Lucretia),

Frankenstein's Lab, where guests can create their own monster (parts supplied), The Belfry Tower, with three different species of bats, and The Dungeon, fully-equipped with the oldest implements and completely sound-proofed.

"Though some of our theme rooms cost an arm and a leg, they're usually the first rented," says Bela, sucking down a glass of what must be red wine.

Their restaurant, called the Witch's Cauldron, has an exciting dinner menu of eyeball soup, lizard tail salad, choice of entrees: freshly-dead brain, batwing stew, cadaver casserole, or roast haunch of hippogriff (the house specialty), dessert of spider-web mousse or chocolate-covered maggots (still moving), finished off by dragon's breath tea. The adjoining lounge, playfully named the Devil's Den, is decorated in hot shades of red and features the Deadly Nightshade Martini and Hellfire Colada.

The inn's repeat business is rare, except for the Count. "Yeah, but he always insists on our cheaper day rate, because he's never in the room at night," grouses Bela.

They accept tour groups, like ghouls & goblins, witches & warlocks, and, during elections, candidates & corpses. Their busiest time of year is Hallowe'en.

The small print at the bottom of their Guest Registration Card is a Double Indemnity insurance clause naming the Toombes as beneficiaries if any guest meets with a sudden "accidental" demise.

Lodging standards are strict, as Lucretia explains: "We won't accept preachers, exorcists, ghostbusters, or computer salespersons - they're bad for business."

Guided haunted walks to nearby cemeteries and derelict mansions can be arranged. "We guarantee that you'll see a ghost - even if it's your own," Bela grins.

Labour concerns don't exist here, Lucretia says. "Our staff are so dedicated, they literally work themselves to the bone."

No matter the season, whatever the reason, the Dead-End Motel welcomes you to a truly life-altering experience. Once you've tried it, you'll never stay anywhere else again. Guaranteed.

*(When alive, I gave my all for this story. Now, my spirit is willing.)*

# IT'S NOT EASY BEING GREEN

*Choose your Hallowe'en costume wisely*

Back in the late 1970s, when disco was king and polyester was fashionable, my wife and I hosted many parties. We especially celebrated Hallowe'en, replete with elaborate macabre decorations, costumes, and the odd zombie (my brother, acting normally). We held our shindigs in the basement of a creepy abandoned house. (We were living with my parents who, to preserve their eardrums from the blaring music, fled their home for the evening.)

One memorable year, when *The Incredible Hulk* was a hit show on TV, yours truly decided to emulate the beast. I figured the Hulk would be an easy costume to make. After all, he was completely naked except for ripped pants. Oh, and his skin was green all over.

I gleefully shredded a pair of old pants, from the thighs on down. At a costume shop, I bought huge plastic feet for "shoes", protecting my real tootsies from the sure-to-be-spilled beer. The costumer also sold me a big tub of emerald green body paint - the Hulk's exact colour. He assured me the paint was easily removable afterwards. My wife recommended I get that assurance in writing, but the shopkeeper had an honest face. Well, except for the scar. And the eyepatch.

On the appointed night, I slathered myself in green body paint. Our guests were quite impressed at being greeted by a snarling Hulk. At least, I think that's what their looks meant.

It was a great party. Batman lusted after Wonder Woman. Richard Nixon boogied with Pierre Trudeau. A convict, whose striped prison outfit came complete with ball and chain, pursued a stunning Playboy bunny. Until his wife, dressed as a cop (with handcuffs), returned him to custody.

Meanwhile, I discovered a major drawback of being painted

green all over: the dye came off, so no one would touch me. No hugs from the ladies (sigh). Even my wife kept her distance; despite being half-Irish, she didn't want green goo smeared on her. Nor could I repose on couch or chair, unless I wanted it stained emerald.

The worst surprise came hours later, after the last guest had dearly departed. Before helping my wife clean up the post-party detritus, I jumped into the shower to banish my green body.

The paint didn't come completely off.

No matter how hard I scrubbed, or how much soap I used, or how hot the water was, my skin stayed green. It just went a lighter shade. Exhausted, despondent, resigned to life as an olive-hued untouchable, I slumped to the shower floor.

My wife had remained sober all evening (unlike me). However, while I spent forever in the shower, she had eaten the gin-soaked orange slices at the bottom of the punch bowl. She was now in a real good mood.

She finally poked her head into the bathroom, wondering if I'd drowned. She exploded into laughter at the sight of The Incredible Hulk transformed into The Pale Green Sulk.

It took her an hour, using a hard floor brush, to get me in the pink again.

"Told ya to get it in writing," she muttered.

"Ouch, ouch, ouch," I replied.

Kermit The Frog was right when he sang: "It's not easy being green".

Years later, I met Lou Ferrigno, the massive bodybuilder who had played the Hulk on TV. I said I empathized with him, being painted green every week, because I had done it once. Giving me a strange look, he said a special cream removed it easily.

Then he grinned a Hulkish grin and charged me $20 for his autograph.

***(I have stayed in the pink ever since.)***

# CELEBRATING BIRTHDAYS

*Casinos outdo relatives with many happy returns*

In my family, all birthdays were carefully arranged to fall within an 11 day period in summer. This was done both for convenience (we just have to remember the first one, then all the others come to mind), and for economy (the same wrapping paper and bow can be reused for all birthdays that year, if the recipients unwrap carefully. We could save even more money with one generic birthday card, but that might be overdoing it).

Grouped birthdays allow our large colourful "Happy Birthday" flag to be raised on our flagpole just once, covering the entire 11 day period. It means that relatives can trek to Peterborough for one all-inclusive birthday visit, saving on gasoline or train tickets. (Here's a riddle only quantum physics can explain: the distance to see us is always longer than the distance we travel to see them.)

However, there is a downside. Some restaurants offer free desserts for the birthday person. For the first birthday, everything is fine. The wait staff present the dessert with smiles, a song, clapping, and a big sparkler atop the confection. But if we return to the same restaurant several days later, celebrating the next birthday, the servers get a little suspicious. The smiles seem forced, the clapping not as hearty, the singing a trifle abrupt. Even the sparkler seems smaller.

When we show up for the third birthday, the manager demands to see a driver's licence or passport to verify the birthday's authenticity. The dessert arrives with a weakly-sputtering stub of a candle. No one sings.

In recent years, we've noticed a curious phenomena. With the proliferation of casinos, we often stop in when we travel through Ontario and Quebec, as a break from the driving and to lighten the load by removing excess weight from our wallets. Naturally, we signed up for each casino's free VIP program, so that all the money we lose can be counted in VIP points which, in 20 years, can get us a free toaster or alarm clock.

The casinos know exactly when our birthdays are, thanks to the documentation they extracted from us to join their VIP program. And here's the phenomena: yearly, we each receive a cheerful birthday card from every casino weeks before our birthday. The cards arrive well before any friend or relative's cards, and the casinos never forget our special day. Sometimes, we even get a present, like $30 in slot tokens if we celebrate our natal day amidst their flashing lights and whirling wheels.

The financial institutions that shanghai whatever money we earn that the Canada Revenue Agency and the casinos don't get, do much the same thing. We receive hearty best wishes by letter or email, weeks before a relative remembers to send an "Oops, sorry!" belated birthday card.

How come casinos and bankers remember your birthday earlier and more consistently than friends and relatives? Perhaps it's because friends and relatives don't have the same incentive as casinos and banks. So maybe we should give family and friends our hard-earned cash, instead.

Why isn't there a Bank of Uncle Joe? Or Aunt Petunia's Casino?

Even better, a one-stop cash grab: Best Buddy Bob's Bank and Casino Emporium, where every Monday you get a free monogrammed bottle opener just for walking in the door?

Boggles the mind. (You can tell my mind is easily boggled.)

*(I love my friends and relatives dearly, especially as my birthday approaches.)*

# Chapter Six

## Pleasures & Pastimes

# GETTING INTO HOT WATER

*The naked truth about spa etiquette*

Three years ago, at the urging of my wife who felt I didn't have enough to do, I became possessed by an outdoor spa. ("Spa", by the way, is a fancy word for "hot tub", meaning a large round or rectangular container full of nearly-scalding water, into which you pour equal parts chemicals, people, and money. Stir until cooked.) Someone possessed by a spa is forced into a weekly routine of checking water, chemicals, temperature, and cursing overflying incontinent birds.

As a public service, I have crafted these Rules of Etiquette for spa users:

★ Don't do anything in a spa that you would not normally do in your backyard. So if you don't garden, or cut the lawn, or sunbathe stark naked, then don't climb in and out of your spa in the buff either. Some of your neighbours may have weak hearts.

★ Please ensure that all bubbles are only generated by the machine. You know what I mean.

★ Verify that your bathing suit is not so old, or of such flimsy construction, that it dissolves in very hot chemicalized water. If the spa is occupied by a bevy of cheerleaders, you may disregard this rule.

★ Soaking in superheated water is detrimental to your health if you stay in too long, like, say, for three hours. Upon exiting, immediately cover yourself with a towel, since your skin will make a prune look smooth.

★ Spas can cause black eyes, or even divorces. Under all those frothing bubbles, make sure you're playing footsie with the right person.

★ Only enter a spa with the owner's permission. It's rude to enjoy someone's spa in the middle of the night, especially if you've never met the owner. Singing ribald songs at the top of your lungs doesn't help.

★ If you notice your spa-less neighbours gawking while you're soaking, cheerfully invite them to join you. For a fee. For their convenience, accept major credit cards.

★ Don't bring foreign objects into the spa with you. Brush grass and dirt from your feet, take a dip in the neighbour's pool first if you're dripping with oily sunscreen (they won't mind; that's what pools are for), and leave the dog on land. Think of the harried spa owner, who must maintain a delicate balance of chemicals in the water you're enjoying. You may ignore this rule if the foreign object is your cute cousin from Ireland.

★ Remove dangling earrings, necklaces, and other jewelry. This rule also applies to women. You don't want to clog the filter. If you ignore this rule, be aware that any jewelry found in the spa becomes the property of the owner. Unless it clashes with his eyes.

★ Please don't splash and *never* jump in. Again, use your neighbour's pool for that. Spas are for quiet relaxation (unless those cheerleaders are still present). If the spa owner must add water while you're still in the tub, it will be *cold*.

★ Remember that TV commercial about the guy in a spa taking Imodium? Not a good thing to talk about while soaking. Ditto any medical problems involving communicable diseases. Talk about the weather.

★ Never block the water intake with your hand, foot, belly, butt, or handy bikini top. It will overheat the motor. You will also run the risk of being severely injured by the owner of the purloined bikini top.

★ Don't overcrowd the spa with loveable plastic animals. Three yellow ducks, two smiling alligators, four laughing dolphins, and a shark that disturbingly resembles our Prime Minister, will be quite enough. Insist that your husband remove his two-foot-long fully-functional submarine.

**(As a partly-functional humourist, I'm all wet.)**

# DARING THE WIND

### *A sailor gets upset*

I've been a sailor since I was a lad. My mother seized upon my youthful interest in sailing as a legal way of getting me out of her sight for extended periods of time, and promptly enrolled me in a sailing club.

There, I learned many colourful nautical terms, usually after tipping my boat and pitching everyone into the drink.

Years later, I was overjoyed to find a girlfriend who shared my passion for sailing. She only had one rule: no tipping. She preferred to stay atop the waves, not in them. It was a small price to pay for romance (and the convenience of having a crew whenever the winds were fair). So I honoured her rule.

Until that fateful day on Chemong Lake.

By then, I had been skippering for decades and my crew had expanded to include our son. I hadn't tipped a boat in all that time. That day, the sun was shining and little whitecaps waltzed across the lake. The winds were brisk-to-gusting, propelling our 14-foot craft up and down the lake at high speed (a rarity for us, since the wind usually died as soon as we set sail). We all wore lifejackets.

We were close-hauled to the wind (for you landlubbers, that means sails pulled tight for maximum speed). Our boat was tilted sharply, bow slicing through the waves with joyous geysers of spray, which soaked my scurvy crew at their positions ahead of me, where they were stationed ostensibly to tend the jib (the small sail in front of the big mainsail) and hike down the boat (balance the boat against the wind) by sitting on the gunwale (edge) and leaning out over the water (the wet part of the lake). Actually, their *real* job was to shield the captain from the spray - but don't tell them!

The wind got stronger. The leeward gunwale (the side opposite the wind) was frequently submerged in the water. We were all hiking hard, my crew holding on to the jib-sheet (line controlling the jib) and the gunwale, while I gripped the main-sheet (line controlling the mainsail) and the tiller (handle controlling the rudder).

My tiller was a beautiful thing: a slender long pole, in gleaming varnish, custom-made from layered oak and mahogany by a marine woodworker in Toronto.

I refused to let out the mainsail, which would have slowed the boat and reduced its tilt. We were holding our own against the strong wind.

Euphoric, I shouted a challenge: daring the wind to do its worst!

There was a loud *crack*. My wife jerked her head around to look, and saw my feet disappear over the side. She just had time to think "he's picked a fine time to go swimming" when the boat, relieved of the (significant) weight of its skipper and with the mainsail suddenly released, flopped hard to windward, tossing my crew into the lake.

My lovely tiller handle had snapped clean off.

I surfaced to see our bright orange hull. The boat had turned turtle (flipped completely upside-down).

My crew surfaced, sputtering, and glared at me accusingly (means mutiny). Ignoring the ancient Captain's Code of Accepting Responsibility, I said it wasn't my fault, it was faulty workmanship.

They didn't buy it.

I then said the boat was perfectly fine when I left it - they were the last ones with it - what happened? (Their response deleted.)

To this day, they blame me for stupidly daring the wind to do its worst.

*(Avast! My mutinous crew has marooned me somewhere uncharted.)*

# I WAS A GARAGE SALE GREMLIN

*Some people should never host garage sales*

In olden days, when folks had far less stuff, things were used until they broke, then carefully repaired, used again, repaired again, then handed down to the next generation to abuse. When things were finally all worn out, they were carted off to the dump.

We don't do that anymore. Now we have garage sales.

These events clearly demonstrate that one family's junk is another's bargain. Garage sales serve a vital societal function: without them, garages and basements would never get cleaned out, causing cramped living conditions, marital strife, cars exposed to the elements, and occasional lost children.

Having co-hosted and co-attended many garage sales, I've observed that they reveal homeowners' innate retailing ability - or lack thereof.

Some sellers take to dealing with the hordes flocking up their driveway like a politician to a photo-op. All smiles and cheery banter, they love interacting with the public.

Other folks rank hosting a garage sale below getting a tooth pulled. They clearly don't like it, can't wait until it's over, then cart their unsold stuff to the dump muttering they'll never waste their time with such nonsense again.

Admittedly, garage sales do come with certain challenges. The weather. Running out of change. Pets and young children not on a leash. Spouses reluctant to sell a dust-shrouded something because "we might need it someday".

Worst challenge of all is the Crack-of-dawn Commandos, who believe the 8:00 am start time in your newspaper ad applies to everyone else. They show up at 6:30 am, when you're bleary-eyed and chugging coffee while hauling your paraphernalia out of the garage and setting up your display tables. They quickly look over your stuff, announce it'll never sell, then graciously offer you a fraction of your price to take it off your hands.

Before they return home to their own garage sale, where they'll cheerfully re-sell your goods at twice what they paid you for it, they scrutinize the other things in your garage, belongings you hadn't intended to sell, and start making you offers. Sometimes, instead of telling these twits to get lost, their offers are tempting, especially if your family was careless enough to leave you alone. For example:

"Oh, that weedwacker over there? (The one you borrowed from your neighbour weeks ago.) Sure, I'll sell it to you for that price. Hey, throw in another $300, and that lawn tractor (also borrowed) is yours too."

"The antique bicycle there? (Which your wife rode as a girl, a gift from her dad, that she's kept for sentimental reasons.) Why, that's a fair amount you're offering. Sold! Here, I'll even help put it in your trunk."

"The canoe hanging from the ceiling? (Once paddled in the same lake canoed by the late Prime Minister Trudeau; surely a valuable future donation to the Canadian Canoe Museum.) Yep, you've got a deal. Let's get 'er strapped to your roof."

"Yes, that snowblower works fine. (Your wife and children will appreciate shoveling snow next winter; it's great exercise, especially since you've just sold their skis.) Sure, I'll take your cheque; you have an honest face."

"Those boxes of old tools? (Which your elderly dad gave you to store until he recovers from his stroke.) Nah, I've got no use for 'em. Make me a good offer and they're yours."

Mind you, afterwards, don't be surprised if you're never allowed to help at a garage sale again.

Which wouldn't necessarily be a bad thing, would it?

*(My family will happily sell me - cheap - at their next garage sale.)*

# ADVENTURES IN SUSHI

*The joys of eating raw fish off almost-nude females*

When some people hear "sushi", they think "raw fish" and immediately go "ugh". A colleague of mine went to Japan on business and almost starved to death.

The purveyors of sushi try to overcome the raw fish stigmata by giving the items exotic names, like Maguro, Sake, Ebi, Hirame, Hamachi, Toro, Uni, Unagi, Ika, and Tako. And when the sushi platter arrives, the items look so appetizing and colourful: bite-sized slivers of fish perched atop small carefully-shaped mounds of rice. Most first-time sushi diners, being adventurous, would simply dip the items in soya sauce and wolf them down, to the delight of their taste buds. But there's always some idiot (me) who insists on reading the English translation of the quaint Japanese names of what's on the platter.

Maguro means tuna. That's not so bad. Tastes great, too.

Sake in this case is not Japanese rice wine, but salmon, which also tastes wonderful.

Ebi is shrimp, and who hasn't enjoyed delicious raw shrimp?

Hirame is flounder and Hamachi is yellow tail, both of which also taste great.

Toro is, er, tuna belly and Uni is, um, sea urchin. Hmmm, well, why not? Down the hatch!

Unagi is eel. Ika is squid. Tako is octopus.

Raw eel. Raw squid. Raw octopus. Um, sounds yummy, doesn't it?

Say, are you turning green? Hey, where are you going?

By this time, any squeamish diners have left, leaving more of the platter for the rest of the group. (Clever, eh?)

My family and I are huge lovers of sushi. And Peterborough is blessed with wonderful sushi restaurants, whose staff know us on sight. ("Ah! It's the Gravels! Quick, I'll distract them by bowing while you check if we have a whale in the fridge!")

Unfortunately, one thing Peterborough will likely never have is almost-nude female sushi platters.

Yes, you read it right. It's quite trendy in some American cities, especially in California where the trend started, to serve sushi atop a supine nearly-naked woman. It's called *nyotaimori,* or "body sushi".

With banana leaves modestly covering a G-string and flowers on her nipples, the living platter lies perfectly still on her back while the sushi chef carefully arranges his creations on her body, then while the diners pick them off with their chopsticks. The chef replenishes the sushi as it's eaten. The woman may talk, but she can't move for hours, nor can she twitch when chopsticks mistakenly pinch her skin while grabbing the sushi. She must take shallow breaths. Sneezing would be disastrous.

So besides California's more famous attractions, there is now another reason to visit Arnold's state.

I doubt such a thing would be allowed in Ontario. Our legions of zealous health inspectors, who after years of terrorizing restaurants are now targeting farmers' markets and church suppers, are very particular about how food is served. Crusaders against bacteria, they have regulations about sterilizing tableware by thorough washing in scalding water. You couldn't do that to a human body. (Although Body Sushi Dishwasher would become a highly-sought-after job for men. In fact, many would do it for free.)

However, if we could work around the health regulations, offering body sushi here would boost our tourism industry. It would be a year-round weather-proof indoor attraction, energy-saving (no cooking), environmentally-sound (no paper plates), with great scenery that would certainly be talked-about when the tourists return home (word-of-mouth is the best advertising - and it's free).

However, I would be banned from such places. I'd have difficulty controlling my chopsticks.

***(Dishonourable Gravel-san has control issues.)***

147~

# TODAY'S WONDER WOMEN

### *Female handypersons take over*

Nowadays, when you want something done around the house, ask a woman.

I don't mean housework, that traditional bane of womankind. These days, females have managed to offload about 20% of the household chores onto men (an equal share by male calculations).

I'm talking about projects: repairs, new construction and renovations.

To fill all that free time from those outsourced chores, women have become the new handypersons. You name it, they're doing it: sanding, painting, cutting, nailing, fastening, fixing, gluing and wrenching.

Handy with all sorts of power tools, especially since manufacturers are making them more suited for smaller hands. Adept with manual tools too: hammer, blowtorch, screwdriver, scraper, paintbrush, pliers. You name it today, and a woman's hand has operated it.

Many women have successfully migrated from their traditional supervisory role (also called criticizing), to hands-on construction. And they're quite good at what they do. They attend how-to sessions at the local hardware store, they read do-it-yourself books and magazines, and - something alien to a male - they read the directions on a product *before* it is applied, not after it's fouled-up.

Home projects performed by women get done much faster than those done by men, because of all the time women save by not nagging the males to get off their lazy butts to do it. And there's no arguments or hurt feelings about how the guy's accomplishments could have been done better; she can do it herself to perfection the first time. (If it's not perfect, her guy better not say otherwise.....)

Women have breached the doors of a traditional male bastion: the hardware store. Half the clientele in today's hardware stores are women. Half the expert sales associates are too.

I've had personal experience with this phenomenon. My wife knows her way around our home's well-stocked workshop as well as me, and has spent as much time, or more, using some of the tools.

For instance, she refinished our entire deck single-handed, stripping and sanding it right down to bare wood, then re-staining and sealing it again. (During the sanding phase, she entered the house caked with hours of sweat and sawdust, looking like she had just crossed the Sahara - twice. Small children fled screaming from the sight of her.)

She can troubleshoot our furnace when it expires on a frigid winter's day, coaxing it back to life more efficiently than copious amounts of my swearing.

She custom-designed four beautiful bookcases, expertly assisted me in their construction (it really is better to measure twice and cut once), and finished them off with a radiant stain. Ditto a queen-size headboard/bookcase and a large pantry/spice cabinet.

She can grout tiles, parge foundations, trowel cement and belch like a contractor.

However, what's truly awesome, is that not only can she do all this formerly-male-type stuff, but she's a wonder in the kitchen too. Her culinary expertise is outstanding, on a variety of dishes, all with a unique taste. (I've long suspected her secret ingredient is sawdust, but have never been able to prove it.)

Now you may wonder: where am I during all this? Well, for example: this past summer I was inside our cool house ostensibly painting a room (I was actually writing this story, but don't tell her), while she was outside in the blazing heat power-sanding nine six-foot Western Red Cedar planks that became our new picnic table. Slathered in aromatic red sawdust, she was happy as a lark.

We had some great-tasting ribs for dinner that night.

***(I changed a lightbulb yesterday - all by myself!)***

# CAUGHT
# IN A MID-LIFE "CAR-SIS"

### *Seduced by exotic models*

I'm being seduced by an exotic female and my wife is okay with that.

The Nissan 350Z, in orange-bronze LeMans Sunset colour. Or the BMW Z4 Roadster. Or any one of a dozen fast and sexy sports cars ranging in price from mid-forties to low-eighties. All convertibles, of course. The literature on these sleek jungle cats all promise similar benefits: "an exhilarating link to the forces of nature." "Responsive performance." "Precise handling." And the Apple that tempted Adam: "unbridled euphoria."

Yep, the symptoms are obvious: I'm suffering from mid-life "car-sis".

Actually, it's not just a male thing. My wife feels it too: the need to buy something frisky, extravagant and *fast*. Something that'll turn people's heads. That only has *two* form-fitting bucket seats, meaning kids are left curbside. That hugs the road tighter than two teenage lovers, letting you experience the sheer joy of cruising, the wind rushing through your hair (well, *her* hair, anyway. Mine went south years ago. If I want wind rushing through my hair, I'd have to drive shirtless, causing my wife to grouse about Ontario laws permitting toplessness).

We've always driven a certain kind of car: *practical*. Station wagons and mini-vans. At times, one of each. His 'n' hers practicalmobiles: versatile - but *dull*. Vehicles adept at hauling teams of kids, fields of plants, forests of lumber, or carts of groceries. With a roof rack for canoe, toboggan, or Christmas tree, and a hitch to haul a trailerful of boat or snowmobile.

Over the decades, we have often been tempted by the siren song of the sports car. Seductive. With come-hither headlights and sexy curves. But we've always resisted, and instead bought the practical conveyance. Which has served us very well; after all, sports cars can't carry much with a trunk the size of a glove compartment and no back seat. They can't pull anything, they drink gas like a Cabinet Minister guzzling booze at taxpayers' expense, cost a fortune to repair and insure, and must be tucked away for the winter.

Lately, however, having passed that "certain age", we've been saying: "Hey, if we don't get that sports car now, then when? We've not getting any younger!"

Why not succumb to the metal-and-leather Jezebel? Our son is grown. Our careers are successful. Interest rates are low, making it easy to do the patriotic thing for our economy and pile on more debt. Isn't this our last chance to buy something *fun*, before we reach that age when legislation requires us to drive a beige sedan?

So we've visited the showrooms. Collected the glossy brochures. Read the consumer reports. And seen the envy in our son's eyes because we might finally buy a car worthy of Bond, James Bond. (Though there's no way he's going to drive it before he's 40.)

We're all set to order one of these powerful panthers, when a neighbour, who's also of a "certain age", tells us he's long been envious of our mini-van and how versatile it is and he's going to buy one because it's great for hauling all sorts of stuff including grandkids with toys.

Huh? Does this mean we've been doing it right all along?

Sighing deeply, we resolve not to be tempted by sports cars any longer. That's over. Finito.

Besides, in honour of the 100th Anniversary of Harley-Davidson, they made a stunning Electra Glide Classic special edition touring motorcycle that's calling out to us with a throaty, seductive rumble...

*(We're still being tempted. Read on for what we finally decided.)*

# MID-LIFE "CAR-SIS":
# THE SEQUEL

*Sir, you're drooling on the chrome*

Readers of the previous story may be wondering: what did we finally decide? Well, since you asked:

On a grey overcast Saturday that definitely needed livening up, we drove to Peterborough's award-winning Nissan dealer, where the powerful 350Z convertible lurked, eager to be unleashed upon a highway. We got intimate with the car, examining every inch, marvelling at this pinnacle of Japanese manufacture.

The test drive was awesome. Though we were hesitant at such a major purchase, the skilled salesperson worked her magic and at the end of the day, we were the proud owners of a Nissan 350Z.

Coffee mug. With cool burnished aluminum highlights, too.

Next weekend, we travelled to the nearest BMW dealer, where we fondled the sleek Z4, selected the exterior and interior colours we liked, and returned home with two peerless examples of precision German engineering: matching BMWs.

Golf shirts. With snazzy embroidered logos.

Forget a diamond ring or fur coat; my wife has always wanted a Jag, with a classic long bonnet ("hood" to us colonials), in British Racing Green. Took me a while, but I finally located a vintage mint-condition 1961 green Jaguar XKE, with a bonnet that stretched on forever, and hand-stitched leather seats. I blew the wad on it; nothing but the best for the love of my life. My wife gave a squeal of joy when I brought it home.

She's always polishing it, making the chrome sparkle like a newlywed's eyes. She looks at it last thing at night and first thing in the morning.

It's on her dresser, the nicest 1:18 scale metal model you've ever seen. The rubber wheels turn, and the bonnet lifts up to reveal that powerful British engine.

After work one day, breathing deep of the crisp fresh air, the sun shining in a cloudless sky of sapphire blue, I visited our excellent local Harley-Davidson store. I spent over an hour ogling the two-wheeled beasts, each one gleaming and obviously yearning to hit the open road with my firm hands on the handlebars and my used-to-be-firm butt on the leather seat. Well, I stayed there so long, I couldn't resist (actually, they ordered me to either buy something or leave, because I was drooling all over their polished machines). So I drove home with my very own Harley.

T-shirt. With awesome designs front and back.

Now before you think all we did was buy shirts, mugs and scale models, last weekend we took delivery of a sparkling new Mustang GT convertible, in canary yellow with chrome wheels. Yep, a for-real automobile: a birthday present for my wife. Our neighbours were so surprised, they interrupted their perpetual-motion yard chores to come gawk at it.

We tried to act nonchalant.

Later, engine purring, we travelled scenic rolling highways and byways all over the Kawarthas, top down, sun shining, the wind in her hair, Tilley hat covering the vacant premises formerly occupied by my hair.

That Mustang turned heads wherever we drove. Parked, it drew crowds like celebrities attract paparazzi.

Come Monday morning, we were really sad when we had to return it to the car rental agency.

*(We still drive practical cars, darn it.)*

# ARE WE THERE YET?

*Road trip checklist: luggage, maps, kids, tranquilizers*

Ah, the family automobile touring vacation. A North American tradition that started in the 1950s when, not coincidentally, thousands of motels were built.

Everyone shares fond memories of those wonderful trips. Dad getting lost and refusing to admit it, or stop to ask for directions, or turn around to retrace his route. Mom valiantly attempting to decipher maps created by drunken cartographers who had never been to the area they're mapping.

Vague road signs (when you could find them at all). Mechanical trouble in the middle of nowhere. No Vacancy signs when you desperately needed a room. Attractions that barely resembled the glowing description in the travel guidebook - or were closed when you finally found them.

And the most fun of all: traveling with the kids.

Two or three squirming Alien Life Forms who, even though they came from the same parents, can't stand each other. Crammed into a back seat which seemed large enough at the start of the trip, but magically shrinks with each day spent on the road. Who perversely delight in annoying each other by whatever means possible. Who fight and argue constantly. Whose cries of "she's touching me!" or "he's hogging the seat!" ring out every five miles.

All part of the sweet music of car travel, along with humming wheels and dad's infuriated refrain: "Knock it off! Don't make me come back there!"

Countless tactics evolved over the decades to keep the little monsters amused: counting Volkswagen Beetles, I Spy, spotting unusual license plates, counting cars of different colours, bathroom breaks every hour, being first to see the cop chasing you because you weren't kidding when you I Spyed that speed trap, memorizing dad's colourful language when said cop departs after giving dad his third ticket of the trip, and memorizing mom's colourful language when she reads the amount of the fine.

Nowadays, of course, parents don't need those silly old ploys. High tech has made travelling with kids a breeze.

Today, the Back Seat Bizarros have a compact DVD player, with a case full of movies to view. At a volume so loud that mom and dad can't hear, much less enjoy, their music up front. And both parents vow to hunt down and kill the "friend" who gave their kids a complete set of every *Simpsons* episode of the past ten years. Months after the trip is over, just hearing the *Simpsons* theme song causes the parents to twitch uncontrollably.

When they tire of watching DVDs, the demon offspring play portable video games, filling the car with the soothing sounds of rapid-fire weapons, explosions, screeching tires, agonizing death cries, and villainous laughter. And those are just the games put out by Disney. Wait until you travel with teenagers and the video games they play.

Put it this way: that police siren breaking the monotony of your driving will sound quite pleasant.

And don't you dare disturb the kids' concentration by pointing out stunning scenery, or historical landmarks, or wildlife. If it isn't on a video screen, they're not interested.

Some parents, congratulating themselves on their cleverness, purchase mini-vans with separate chairs in the rear. A seat for each child. Guaranteed no fighting.

Doesn't work. They still fight. Should have spent the money on tranquilizers. For the kids. That's how high-strung horses are transported.

But one thing hasn't changed: that familiar whining lament, without which there simply wouldn't be a family road trip:

"Does tonight's motel have Internet?"

*(In my youth, I was left behind several times at rest stops. Deliberately.)*

# WHAT
# AM I BID FOR THIS HUSBAND?

*Why I'm banned from attending auctions*

Some things should never go together, because it always leads to trouble, like: "religious" and "fanatic", or "politician" and "promise", or "teenagers" and "kissing".

Or "me" and "auctions".

In recent years, my wife has taken to attending country auctions, featuring coloured glass collectibles. These quaint rural events are a marvel to experience: right before your eyes, someone's castoffs are transformed into someone else's treasures. Especially if your spouse buys them.

A bewildering hodge-podge of stuff is on display: furniture, tools, appliances, toys, collectibles, machinery, and antiques of every sort. Kind of like what's already crammed into your attic, basement and garage, except no one's bidding on it. Yet.

Also on display are the people. You can easily pick out the professional auctionauts: they look serious, talk among themselves in low whispers, are on a first name basis with the auctioneer and, during the pre-auction examination of items, never show interest in the pieces they want. Until you show an interest, whereupon they glare at you, as if you're fingering something they already own.

Then there are the wide-eyed hopefuls, like my wife, eager to discover an unexpected treasure, and trusting in a fair bidding war conducted by an unbiased auctioneer. Which is what happens, most times.

Lastly, there are those who should never attend auctions. Like me.

Because of my French-Canadian heritage, I tend to talk with my hands, which is an asset when I'm teaching, but a severe liability when auctioning.

Auctioneers, with eyes like hawks and mouths like runaway locomotives, pick up subtle signals from the audience during bidding. Also not-so-subtle signals, like some twit gesturing with his hands as he talks to his wife about the item being bid upon.

Once, I almost purchased a woman's antique dress-making form, before my wife realized what was occurring and quickly ordered me to sit on my hands.

On another occasion, I was one gavel bang away from owning a tub of rusty bicycle sprockets, with a box of rusty bicycle chains thrown in as a bonus.

Then there was that old milking machine that nearly came home with us, with hoses and stainless steel attachments that looked like a monstrous 1950s beauty salon hair curler for the Bride of Frankenstein - and me never having owned a cow.

Though I came close, once.

Years ago, we attended the Calgary Stampede and, eager to soak up the whole western cowboy experience, sat in on a cattle auction. We learned about many different breeds that afternoon - and almost learned too much about one particular cow.

During an intense bidding war for a prize Limousin heifer, my wife finally perceived in horror that, thanks to my hand movements, I was one of the bidders - the most active bidder, in fact. She hauled my arms down just before the gavel banged in my favour, earning an annoyed glare from the auctioneer (already suspicious of us, since we were the only ones not wearing cowboy hats).

My wife now rarely allows me at auctions. She's already under enough stress: watching for a favorite piece to finally come up for bid, then bidding, while guarding her box of acquisitions from jerks trying to paw through it when she's distracted (successful bidders are recorded as owning the items; they must pay for them when leaving, whether still in their possession or not).

Besides, it's best if I don't go. One day she might decide to auction off a clued-out, one-owner husband.

*(My wife is now accepting bids.)*

# CHOCOLATE
# CARIBBEAN CONUNDRUM

*Practical jokes on the high seas*

Something is wrong in our fair city: many people fly south for the winter, while many Canada Geese stay here. Seeking an explanation for this strange behavior, my family and I flew south this past winter and embarked on a Caribbean cruise. I learned a few things.

On the spice island of Grenada, where they have a history of shooting the Prime Minister and his entire Cabinet, there is no mail delivery in rural villages. Instead, residents are expected to trek to their village Post Office to collect their mail. Many people don't, because the mail invariably contains bills and who wants those?

Smart people.

On the isle of St. Kitts, blessed with friendly people and an unemployment rate unheard-of in Canada (only 1%), I spied a pirate flag that proclaimed: "The beatings will continue until morale improves." I immediately bought it to display in my office. My employees seem much happier now.

On a small boat en route to great snorkeling off St Johns, USVI, the captain announced we should be concerned if we saw him donning a life jacket and leaping overboard. This skipper had no intention of going down with his ship because, in his words: "A sinking ship has no need for a captain".

This same captain also admonished us to keep a tight grip on our hats as he sped through the aquamarine Caribbean sea, because: "The only hat we will stop for is one with a head in it".

Working in the hospitality industry as I do, my heart goes out to the Cruise Director of the gigantic floating hotel we called home for a week. Besides the daily challenges of keeping 3,000 disparate passengers happy and entertained every day, he also had to deal with some goofball questions.

Here is a sampling of actual questions asked by people who, I hope, are rational, sober and productive members of society back home:

"Does the ship generate its own electricity?" (No, we're trailing a giant extension cord behind us, all the way from San Juan.)

"Does the crew sleep on board?" (No, they commute to work each day.)

Ship toilets flush with a loud, aggressive suction, inspiring this question: "What happens if I sit on the toilet when I flush it?" (You'd have one helluva time explaining that hicky, buddy.)

A toilet-obsessed passenger asked: "Is the water in the toilet fresh water or salt water?" (You taste it and let me know.)

"If the souvenir pictures taken by the ship's photographers don't have your name or cabin number on them, how do we tell which ones are ours?"

"Is this island surrounded by water?"

"What happens to the ice sculptures when they melt?"

And my personal favorite: "Which elevator do I take to get to the front of the ship?"

*Warning:* if you sail with your piratical kin, beware of practical jokes. Like someone secretly relocating the mint chocolate wafer the cabin steward places on your pillow every night, to the middle of your bed between the sheets. Next morning, when you awake and fling back your sheets, eager to enjoy another glorious day in paradise, you are horrified to see brown splatters beneath you. Hugely embarrassed, wondering if the on-board gift shop sells Depends (they do), you are then assaulted with gales of laughter and endless teasing.

Just try convincing your steward that it's really chocolate stains.

My new family nickname? "Popi Poopy Pants".

It's a damn shame keelhauling and flogging are no longer practiced.

***(I'm the scourge of at least two of the seven seas.)***

# HAVE SHORTS, WILL TRAVEL

*Cultural differences bedevil travellers*

Articles appear regularly in newspapers, extolling the virtues and benefits of travel. It's good for the soul, relaxing (once you finally reach your destination), broadens both mind and waist, and keeps bankers and travel agents off welfare. Travel also exposes you to different cultures, and that's often its best benefit. However, some cultural differences are completely unexpected.

Prior to a business trip to Japan, I prudently read up on local customs, do's and don'ts, business etiquette, and how to ask where the bathroom is in Japanese. I landed confident that I was fairly well-prepared, and my business dealings went along swimmingly.

But on my one day off, when I changed into casual wear for some sightseeing in that humid country (Tilley shorts, short-sleeved shirt, and hat), I couldn't understand why all the women were discretely giggling at me behind their hands, while the men were frowning. I checked my fly constantly; it was always up. What gives?

Next day, back in business attire, I asked my Japanese host about this. Once I described how I had dressed, he broke into loud guffaws. Seems Japanese adult males never ever wear shorts in public, exposing their knees. I'd been touring around Tokyo giving the locals some great entertainment. Well! That was not in any of my guide books. And what was so wrong with my knees anyway? They weren't that knobby.

When I returned the following year, on my sightseeing day, I dressed exactly the same way. This time, I drew round smiley faces on my kneecaps with a magic marker.

Even in the United States, whose culture has many similarities to ours, there are differences. On a trip to Vegas, my wife and I jumped in a cab and said we had 20 minutes to get through cross-town traffic before our theatrical performance started. The cabbie eagerly accepted the challenge, rocketing along a bypass and side roads, sometimes taking corners on two wheels. Approaching one intersection with pedestrians crossing our path, we were horrified when the cabbie sped up, bearing down mercilessly on the people, while laying into his horn. We shot by the startled pedestrians at warp speed, barely missing them.

"My God!" I blurted. "It's not worth killing someone just to get us to our show on time!"

"It's their fault," replied the cabbie. "They were crossing against the light. In Nevada, it's legal to hit someone who's jaywalking. In fact, you're allowed to sue them, or their next of kin, for damages to your car caused by their bodies. They were legitimate targets of opportunity."

"Um, you were in the armed forces, weren't you?" I ventured.

"Yeah, Marines. How'd you guess?"

My son's college roommate returned to the Bahamas, his native land, for Christmas vacation. He and some friends drove to a party, stupidly drinking beer in the car, despite the Bahamas having a drinking and driving law like Canada's.

Well, not exactly like Canada's.

When they were pulled over by a cop, who had spied the driver taking a swig, my son's roommate was aghast, envisioning a Christmas behind bars. The officer ordered the lads to finish their beers then and there, and give him the empties before proceeding on their way.

"There's no drinking and driving in this country," the constable intoned sternly.

Concerning cultures, as the French say: "Vive la difference!"

*(I try to blend in when travelling. I always fail miserably.)*

# HOWDY, DAVY-SAN

*A trilogy of tall travel tales*

It's amazing how American popular culture has spread around the world.

During a business trip to Japan, I used my day off to visit Tokyo Disneyland. Being a big Disney fan, and having visited the two Disney theme parks in the U.S.A., I was intrigued to see how Mickey & Co. had translated over to this Asian culture.

I found much of it was exactly the same, except the hordes of visitors were decidedly Japanese: people were extremely courteous in the line-ups, with no pushing or cutting-in or complaining. It was very weird to hear the familiar Disney songs with Japanese lyrics. It was pleasant to receive - and return - a bow whenever you bought something.

But the most unusual experience was walking along the boardwalk next to the lake in Frontierland, watching an approaching Davy Crockett freight canoe full of passengers, with Davy lookalikes paddling at the bow and stern, replete in coonskin caps and fringed buckskins. An authentic scene right out of American frontier history.

Until the canoe docked, and I saw that both paddlers had the distinctive facial features of Japanese men. It was totally incongruous with their Crockett costumes; ol' Davy never looked like that!

This next tale was related to me by Stuart Harrison, General Manager of Peterborough's Chamber of Commerce. Years ago, on a Mexican vacation with his wife, Stu kept noticing a distinctive bat-shaped emblem on various items in the shops in town. The symbol was on glassware, on t-shirts, sometimes carved in wood. Curious, Stu wondered what that design represented in the local Mayan culture. A religious icon? A national emblem? An ancient

Mayan crest?

Finally, unable to contain himself any longer, he gingerly approached a shopkeeper, asking her:

"Tell me, por favor, what significance does the bat have to your local culture?"

"Huh?" replied the young woman warily, wondering if this gringo had sampled too much tequila.

"I keep seeing that bat symbol on everything," persisted Stu. "It must hold some deep meaning in your culture. What is it?"

"You want to know what is that design, senor?"

"Si," said Stu. "It's quite dramatic."

She laughed: "It is yours, senor, from your land. It is the symbol of Batman!"

A great guy, unfortunately Stu had, up to that point, led a somewhat sheltered life.

On vacation in Aruba, an island as far south in the Caribbean as you can go before smacking into Venezuela, my wife and I debarked the plane and collected our luggage, giving thanks to the travel gods that our bags had actually landed with us.

We passed through Customs and came out into the Arrivals foyer of the terminal, Typical of airports worldwide (except Hamilton), the foyer was packed with people waiting for loved ones, friends and clients. I noticed a neatly-dressed woman with a blinding smile holding a sign sporting an "Abbott" logo. I knew full well that it referred to the multinational pharmaceutical company, but I simply couldn't resist. (Hey, it had been a long flight - and no, I wasn't drunk.) She looked at me hopefully as I approached. I returned her cherubic smile and said:

"Sorry, I'm with Costello."

She groaned, but some of my fellow passengers chuckled. My long-suffering wife, on the other hand, rolled her eyes and pretended she didn't know me.

Which is what she usually does when we're on vacation.

***(I'm quite a handful when I travel.)***

# COFFEE, TEA, OR
# NAKED FRAULEINS?

*Fringe benefits while travelling*

People have asked if I had more true travel tales. Thanks for asking, both of you. Here goes:

Visiting the Dominican Republic, we stayed at a new resort in a remote part of the country. Though eager to please, the staff were obviously hospitality neophytes.

A tea drinker since birth, my wife believes the hotter the water, the better cuppa it makes. If the water sears the enamel off the cup, it's acceptable.

At our first breakfast after arrival, she asked for hot tea. The Spanish-speaking waiter, who knew little English, presented her with a tall glass filled with ice cubes floating in a murky brown liquid with white tendrils of cream. She graciously said she wanted hot tea, not ice tea. The waiter left and reappeared with a coffee mug with a tea bag in it and a glass of warm water straight from the tap.

Next morning, my wife took the waiter aside and explained the proper mechanics of tea preparation, stressing that the water must be furiously boiling before being poured. And a dedicated tea cup would be nice.

Lo! A tea cup was unearthed and placed before her. Water that we were assured had been boiled was poured into it. With a flourish, the tea bag was inserted. She added cream, took a sip, and made a horrible grimace. He had used an unrinsed coffee pot to boil the water.

On Day Three, she received a full mug of hot cream with a tea bag floating in it. She smiled, thanked the waiter, and thumped her head down on the table. Twice.

After breakfast, she signed up for the resort's Spanish lessons and insisted the instructor first teach her how to order a proper cuppa.

On a business trip to Frankfurt, back when hair camouflaged my radar dome, I stayed at an airport hotel. After a long day, I went to the hotel's indoor pool late at night for a swim. I was the only one in the men's change room. I had changed into swim trunks, closed my locker, and turned towards the pool door, when two trim, blonde and well-endowed women opened it, greeted me cheerfully in German, and sashayed into the men's sauna.

They were topless. Not much on the bottoms either.

I dashed to the door. The plaque on the outside read "Herren" (men). Relieved I hadn't gone into the ladies' change room by mistake, I entered the pool which, thankfully, had cold water.

After swimming, I used my halting German to ask the attendant why two almost-naked women were sweating away in the men's sanctum. He explained that the women's sauna was broken, that the ladies were Lufthansa flight attendants and, if I understood his German correctly, he wished me an absolutely wonderful time in the sauna.

The sauna door cracked open as I re-entered the change room and I was invited inside to warm myself. Being a happily married man and wishing to remain so, I politely declined. The sauna door opened wider and I saw that the ladies were now completely starkers.

Ruining a perfect Playboy fantasy, I grabbed my clothes and fled to my room in my wet bathing suit.

Incidentally, I had placed my glasses in my locker right after I had changed, so all I ever saw were fuzzy shapes.

Honest.

*(I now wear my glasses at all times.)*

# DANCES WITH DOLPHINS

### *It must be my animal magnetism*

Last winter, desperate to escape the cold and snow, my family, a friend and I eloped to the warm sunny Caribbean. There, I had an affair. Her smile was winsome; her body was lithe, curvaceous and she moved like a dream.

We embarked on a cruise, which visited several picturesque islands, each fully equipped with the requisite gorgeous beaches and virtually-naked sunbathers (photos available for a reasonable fee).

On the isle of Tortola, in the British Virgin Islands (home of the legendary Pusser's Outpost, whose incredible rum and Caribbean Jerk Pizza is a tale in itself), we had the great fortune to swim with dolphins.

Hence my affair.

Dolphins are sleek, beautiful creatures of high intelligence. (Yet they're indiscriminate about whom they swim with. Me, for instance.) Our encounter took place at a facility specializing in training dolphins to tolerate humans in a controlled environment. The place has high standards of cleanliness and veterinary care, and the energetic mammals have a large natural cove to call home.

As we entered the cove's turquoise water, hearts pounding (not with excitement, but because of the unexpectedly-cold water), a graceful female named Venus swam over to check us out. I was instantly smitten. And I could tell she was attracted to me (perhaps it was the chopped fish in my pocket).

The trainer instructed us on how to kiss Venus. It involved the precise placing of hands to form a small platform, upon which the dolphin would place her snout, whereupon you were supposed to kiss it on the tip.

I had the honour of going first. Venus glided up and placed her snout upon my hands, awaiting her smooch.

Up close, her grinning mouth was a lot bigger than I expected. I suddenly remembered it was filled with needle-sharp teeth. And that sharks, even Great Whites, are terrified of dolphins.

My paramour's dark eyes gazed deep into mine. A sigh of impatience escaped from her blowhole. The trainer urged me to consummate the tryst. Seems the rest of our group also desired some quality time with Venus. (I wasn't jealous; I knew it was me she really wanted.)

Ever debonair, I bypassed her snout and planted a big wet one on her cheek. Then I cuddled my cheek against hers and emulated her beatific smile. The facility's photographer snapped our picture just then, and later consented to part with it for a piratical fee. My family claims the photo perfectly captures the sublime moment of dolphin/goof oneness.

Overcome with my suaveness, Venus then danced with me. As she lifted herself straight up with her strong tail, I grabbed both her flippers and, doing a frog-kick because my own tail had regretfully been evolved away millennia ago, we boogied while the group cheered. (When you dance with a dolphin, the female definitely leads.)

But the best was yet to come.

Venus swam past me, upside down, and again allowed me to grasp both flippers. With me on her smooth white belly and grinning like an idiot (that comes naturally), she towed me the entire width of the cove at high speed, using just her powerful tail.

It was an enthralling experience. I don't know why our proto-ancestors ever emerged from the oceans. Why trade co-habiting with such graceful creatures for snarled highways, mega-malls and mortgages?

Alas, our affair ended way too soon. As a send-off, Venus gave the other humans a friendly wave of a flipper.

I got splashed in the face.

Just her way of being coquettish.


**(Easily-seduced and all wet, I'm now taking marriage counseling.)**

# OF PIRATES AND PARROTHEADS

*Buffetted about in Margaritaville*

To celebrate our 30th wedding anniversary, and being big fans of singer Jimmy Buffett, we decided to do something we've never done before: see him in concert. Jimmy's songs paint images of sailing azure seas, strolling white sand beaches, sipping frosty tropical drinks (especially margaritas), and they celebrate the pirate in us all. So we anticipated a mellow, funky concert experience. The concert date closest to our anniversary was at the MGM Grand Hotel's Garden Arena in Las Vegas.

Jimmy's fans are called "parrotheads". When both we and the big day arrived in Vegas, I donned an authentic parrothead Hawaiian shirt and my honey wore a Margaritaville sweatshirt. (I'd left my stuffed parrot's head cap at home; I didn't want to overdo it.)

The first inkling that the evening would turn out different than expected, was seeing the other fans filing into the arena. We were underdressed. People wore day-glo surfer jams and flip-flops. Men in hula skirts, topless except for polished coconut brassieres. Many folks wore outlandish headgear inspired by Jimmy's songs, like huge parrots with four-foot tail feathers. Straw sombreros festooned with paper drink umbrellas and miniature palm trees. Three-foot-high shark fins, constructed from the narrow balloons clowns use. Some heads carried the entire animal: large plush sharks with tails straight up in the air and distended toothy jaws hungrily gripping the craniums.

Everyone carried a drink. Or two.

We were barely seated when our pre-show entertainment docked at their seats, directly in front of us: the Pirate and Shark-Boy. Caucasian, the Pirate sported massive dreadlocks, bandana, and a hat stolen from Blackbeard. Huge round earrings dangled on either side of his sweaty face, the rims of his battery-powered fluorescent sunglasses flashed 3-D colours, and each hand death-gripped a foaming beer.

His shipmate, Shark-Boy, had a respectable beer-gut, which clashed with his hula skirt and coconut bra ensemble. A shark was painted on his belly, and he showed everyone how he could make it swim.

The Pirate cheerfully introduced his boarding party to all within earshot of his booming voice, then announced we'd better get used to him standing up, because he always danced throughout Jimmy's shows.

The vast 17,000-seat cavern was completely sold out, jammed with well-lubricated parrotheads. Inflatable beach balls were gleefully batted among the crowd. Lightweight basketball poles with hoops wandered the arena, strapped to people's backs, and the audience cheered whenever a beach ball made a basket.

I was bravely preparing to fire a broadside at the Pirate, demanding he sit down once Jimmy appeared, when the lights dimmed and the loudest music I'd ever heard blasted into my skull, ricocheted around my brain, and tap-danced on my back molars. Jimmy Buffett bounded on stage, barefoot, a huge grin on his tanned face.

Everyone stood up. And stayed standing throughout the entire concert.

To say it was a wild experience would be an understatement. To say we danced to the music would be a lie. No one danced; our feet were stuck to the floor thanks to the spilled drinks from the higher rows. We all kinda swayed in place.

"Some mellow Caribbean experience, eh?" I screamed at my wife over the eardrum-shattering music.

She heard: "So, marshmallow coconut sex today?" and slapped my face.

Jimmy obviously had fun entertaining the rabid multitude, as I said two days later when our hearing returned.

We plan a quieter, saner celebration for our next milestone: hosting a birthday party for preschoolers.

*(I'm wasting away in Peterboroughville.)*

# CLOSE ENCOUNTERS
# ON THE TRAIL

*Ever see a tree growing out of a cyclist's back?*

Like other communities across Canada, ours owes a great debt of gratitude to our local Rotarians.

Among the many accomplishments of these dedicated volunteers, is the 50 km Rotary Greenway Trail they created over old railway lines, linking Peterborough with the villages of Lakefield to the north and Omemee somewhere to the west. The trail is used by cyclists, runners, walkers, rollerbladers and, usually in winter, cross-country skiers.

As part of my failing efforts to stay in shape, I often ride my bike up and down the 9 km section of the Trail between Peterborough and Lakefield. It traverses peaceful countryside, offering vistas of farms, the Otonabee River, woodlands and marshes. And sometimes, very unusual sights...

Cycling along one sunny Sunday, I passed a fellow pedaler going in the opposite direction, a too-healthy-looking twentysomething man. With a tree growing out of his back. Concerned that prolonged exposure to the sun was making me hallucinate, I jammed on my brakes and looked back. The cyclist had a four-foot-tall sapling, bagged roots and all, strapped to his back. Maybe the guy was an ardent environmentalist who felt the tree needed some exercise?

On another day, I was resting mid-way up the trail, when two young ladies passed me, chattering away like excited chipmunks discovering an abandoned bag of peanuts. I was taking a long swig from my water bottle as they rode by, and almost choked. One of the women, bent over her handlebars, was showing the world most of her bare backside above her very-low-riding jeans. Though it was late morning, the moon was definitely out.

From time to time, we cyclists have to deal with drunken dogs. Most dogs using the trail pace in a straight line alongside their masters, so that oncoming cyclists can safely pass to one side. However, some dogs, obviously inhabited by the soul of a former drunken sailor, tack from side to side across the trail. This makes passing the zig-zagging critter quite challenging. Their masters are no help at all, except to berate the hapless cyclist for narrowly missing their spirit-possessed pet.

Children using the trail sometimes exhibit the same zig-zagging behavior, leading me to suspect that this area is rife with reincarnated sailors.

Towards the end of each summer, after cycling regularly since spring, I fool myself into believing I've achieved fair aerobic shape. By then, I can do the entire length of the trail without a break, and I also significantly cut the time it takes to get from here to there and back again.

One fine day last September, I was zooming along making my best time ever, the wind whistling, wheels humming lustily, the countryside zipping by. I was going flat out and it felt wonderful. A swell of pride filled me. Not bad for a guy who's seen over half a century go by! Wah-hoo!

Then something else went by: a female university student (property of Trent, according to her skin-tight cycling shorts) with thighs thick as tree trunks. She passed me from behind like I was standing still.

Shocked, I coasted to a stop, watching her zip down the trail at warp speed until she was but a dot in the distance. I felt like the coyote in those Road Runner cartoons, with my jaw falling to the ground in astonishment.

Young people today - they should be more careful around older folk with fragile egos. Ought to be a law.

*(Since then, I rarely feel proud when I go cycling.)*

# MY SUMMER CONCUSSION

*Getting attention - the hard knocks way*

To flamboyant chef Emeril Lagasse, BAM! means "kick it up a notch" when cooking. To me, it means something else.

Some people do strange things to get attention. They pose for family photos wearing red clown noses. They enter politics or become comedians (same thing). Some pathetic souls write humour stories.

Me? I crack my head open. Once a year, in summer. Always gets great laughs.

Mind you, I'm no masochist. I don't injure myself deliberately. It happens naturally.

The first time it happened was three years ago, when I was launching our boat. To keep my feet dry, I perform acrobatic maneuvers worthy of Cirque du Soleil. People around the dock watch, mouths agape. My First Mate sells tickets.

I open the rear liftgate of our van, back up until the rear wheels and the entire boat trailer are in the water, climb through the van, inch out along the trailer tongue to the bow of the boat, then push it free. Turning, I gingerly walk the balance beam of the tongue back to the van and re-enter through the open liftgate.

I'd performed this trick flawlessly many times - until that fateful day when I didn't duck low enough for my head to clear the liftgate edge as I flung myself back into the van.

**BAM!**

Ouch. To put it mildly. I'd been wearing my Tilley hat with a Canadian flag pin in front, and the impact rammed the back clamp of the pin into my bald head, which then scraped along to the back of my head as I went forward, giving me a nasty foot-long scrape. Had to wear a ball cap to work so the scabrous thing wouldn't gross people out. The accident demonstrated that patriotism sometimes calls for suffering.

The second time was almost exactly a year later. We were boating miles from home and a heavy rainstorm caught us. We hastily erected our low canvas canopy over the cockpit, with all its poles and straps. It works great as long as everyone stays seated. We returned to port and stood up to enact our practiced docking routine. Except that I was used to a boat without a top.

**BAM!**

My chrome dome whacked into the crossbar of the canopy. I promptly sat down, to better appreciate the wonderful show of little blue birdies dancing around my eyes. I sported an ugly wide scrape for weeks thereafter. Back to the ball cap for work.

Not being totally stupid (though getting there thanks to regular head trauma), I became extra-cautious around anything nautical. Naturally, the following year, the next accident had nothing to do with boats.

I was helping my college-going son move into a new apartment. As rain was forecast, we prudently rented a hard-top U-Haul trailer. After placing some stuff at the front of the trailer, I crouched low walking back to the open rear doors and stood up as I exited.

**BAM!**

Stood up too soon. Hit the edge of the trailer roof. More little blue birdies. Another painful dent in the noggin. Which later swelled-up real good with lots of pretty colours.

What's left of my intellect has detected a pattern: these accidents have occurred three summers in a row. So all this summer, I'm wearing a construction worker's hard hat whenever I go out. I don't care how ridiculous I look.

Besides, some people will do anything for attention.

*(I barely possess enough undamaged brain matter to administer a non-profit tourism association and write this stuff.)*

# LURING LADY LUCK

*How gamblers try to influence slot machines*


I've been known to visit casinos on occasion. (The Problem Gambling Helpline number is *not* on my cell phone speed-dial. That's an unsubstantiated rumour.) Inside those dens of voluntary taxation, I find the slot machines highly entertaining. Not just the devices' colourful lights, dramatic graphics, and alluring sounds. Equally entertaining are the people who sit before them.

Despite many articles certifying that slot machines are cold sophisticated computers programmed for random selection of winning numbers, many folks persist in believing that their own personal "system" can influence the slots. Or, at least, can influence Lady Luck to grant them a winning spin.

I've observed many quirky habits.

Some players stroke their machine, passing their hands over the buttons and chrome, or over the glass window in front of the spinning dials, or over absolutely everything.

The method of stroking varies with the gambler. Some move their hands slowly, like caressing a lover or a sleek sports car (same thing). Others stroke rapidly, like a rabid diner attacking a buffet table, anxious to get something from every station before someone else does.

Then there are the folks who stroke in a set pattern, either zigzag, or up and down, or in a circle. Some people perform a complicated pattern combining all three motions. While patting their head. Touching their nose with the tip of their tongue helps too.

One gambler fondles the knob atop the pull-lever at the side of the machine. Another rubs the seat of the chair. After first walking around it three times, counter-clockwise. (Little does she know that manoeuver never works unless you also cluck like a chicken.

Trust me.)

Some feed money into a machine until it gets "hot": granting modest wins most of the time. If that player must leave to answer a call of nature or have a smoke, they take extraordinary measures to prevent anyone else playing "their" machine in their absence, lest the hot streak be broken. They place coin buckets over the controls, tilt the chair up against the machine, or prop a sign on it. They'd ring it in yellow "do not cross" police tape if they could get some. I saw one guy sternly instruct his wife to stand guard over "his" machine, but not to touch it whatsoever, or else his luck would be broken. Then off he dashed.

As soon as he was out of sight, she touched the machine. With a big smile.

Some hum a tune to their machine. Others talk to their slot: cordially, or authoritatively, or cajoling, or pleading. Some gamblers treat their machines indifferently, casually, like long-married couples. Instead, they wear "lucky clothing", or eat a "lucky meal" beforehand, or send a fervent prayer heavenward (fulfilling that request has got to be far down on God's to-do list, even below a teen's plea for a zit-free face, or a mayor's wish for a cooperative council).

A friend of ours works at a casino, and he confided that some patrons have even more bizarre mannerisms. He divulged the most disgusting habit: people who lick their coins before inserting them in the machine. Yuck! Now I know why many slot parlours have switched from coins to paper chits.

I don't do any of those silly (and unsanitary) shenanigans. I sit down, play the machine, and it does what it does.

Now please excuse me while I go look for my lucky piece of chewing gum. Been gnawing the same wad for over six years. I'm convinced it'll really pay off one day.

Any day now.

**(I've watched way too many spinning dials.)**

# FLY LIKE AN EAGLE

### *Land like a dodo*

Decades ago, when I was young and stupid (I'm no longer young), I attended McGill University in Montreal. All of 18, caught up in the heady freedoms of new adulthood, I craved unique experiences. Already a scuba diver, I reasoned that if I enjoyed soaring through the underwater world, then surely I would enjoy soaring through the abovewater world. So I took up skydiving.

My girlfriend thought I was nuts. My parents knew I was nuts.

I joined the McGill Skydiving Club. They promptly unveiled a long legal liability document for me to carefully read and sign. Eager to soar like an eagle, I used the brains of a dodo and signed with barely a glance at the close-packed type.

I paid more attention in skydiving class - especially the lecture on What To Do If Your Chute Doesn't Open - and took many notes. (My girlfriend asked what good would my notes do when I was two miles up, falling at over 140 feet a second. Good point.)

The Big Day finally arrived. My first jump. My honey, muttering that sane people did not voluntarily leap out of perfectly good airplanes, accompanied me to a small airport north of Montreal.

We were a mixed group: ebullient would-be skydivers with somber friends who looked like their next stop would be a funeral (highly probable). Clad in jumpsuits, outfitted with our main and spare parachutes, checked and cross-checked, four of us eager eaglets crammed into a modified Cessna with the pilot and instructor. The plane lumbered skyward.

En route to the drop zone, a curious phenomena occurred: the higher we climbed, the less excited we got. Finally, the cabin door was latched open and, with a demonic grin, the instructor selected me to go first. Pushing forward against the buffeting wind, remembering stern warnings not to look down, I emerged from the cabin's safe womb and inched along a ledge under the wing, hands death-gripping the wing strut.

The instructor screamed: "GO!"

I screamed: "WHY? Haven't I already demonstrated my courage just by exiting this aircraft at 2,000 feet?"

The instructor reminded me that returning to the cabin was not an option. It was too hazardous. (Like letting go wasn't hazardous???)

The instructor was implacable. I let go.

Arms and legs spread wide, arching my body backward like we'd been taught, I fell away.

Then the idiot-cord attached from the plane to my chute snapped tight and, miracle of miracles, my chute flowed out behind me. Even more miraculous, it ballooned open. Straps jerked tight, I was yanked upright and voila: I floated over serene Quebec farmland.

Awesome view: blue sky around me, white canopy above, green fields below. Green fields coming closer every second. With mysterious brown spots on them. That moved.

I was coming down on a field full of cows.

I pulled on the chute cords, attempting to change direction. That just moved me from the edge of the field to the middle. Where the cows were thickest. I figured that Bessy would not take kindly to someone suddenly dropping onto her back from above. I yelled down at the herd, to get them to move. They stayed put. Remembering they were Quebecois bovines, I bellowed in french. Same result.

I just missed a cow as I landed and rolled, shouting "Merde!", which accurately described what I landed in. The animal, eyes bulging in astonishment, bolted.

My chute settled gracefully behind me. Upon the rest of the herd. Chaos ensued.

*(My second jump was also my last. Read the next story to see if I survived.)*

# THE EAGLE HAS PLOTZED

*What goes up, comes down badly*

You just read of my first skydiving jump, done in the early 1970s when I was a university student with an acute shortage of common sense. This tale is of my second - and last - jump.

My first time, I came to roost in a pasture full of cows, almost landing on one of them. My girlfriend and parents thought that close call would have dissuaded me from further leaps of faith.

They thought wrong.

Determined to soar again, I paid no heed to their dire "what if" scenarios, like: "Next time, what if you land on a busy highway, or in a lake, or in a forest?"

My brother, equally concerned for my welfare, added: "What if you die or become horribly crippled - can I have your motorcycle?"

They remained unconvinced when I said I knew what I was doing.

So, two weeks later, there we were again at that small airport north of Montreal, with the same group of excited skydivers and gloomy friends. (Actually, the number of repeat skydivers had dwindled significantly after their first jump, an observation my girlfriend made - repeatedly.)

Once again, four bird-brains piled into the Cessna and off we went into the wild blue yonder.

This time, I was picked to jump last (the instructor remembered my reluctance to let go once I'd inched out under the wing). When it was my turn, determined to repair my reputation, I wasted no time clambering out and letting go. A textbook display of macho. (I'm sure he didn't hear my whimpering over the roar of engine and wind.)

My chute again blossomed open, a rather fortunate occurance.

The straps bit into the youthful body beneath the jumpsuit as I was hauled upright. I stopped screaming and enjoyed the wonderful view as I floated over the countryside.

There was no sound except for the wind, whistling through my empty head. It was intensely serene.

Then I remembered what went up inevitably must come down. I looked to where the wind was sending me. (Trainer parachutes are quite unresponsive compared to more expensive, advanced chutes. With those, you could literally control your descent to land on a dime. With my chute, you couldn't land on the Canadian Mint if it was right below you.)

Only empty fields lay beneath me. Not a cow in sight. I heaved a sigh of relief.

Dropping lower, I observed that the local farmers had industriously bordered their fields with lines of sturdy upright posts holding up miles of wire fence.

One of those sturdy upright posts was directly below me, framed between my dangling feet.

I was about to be impaled. Bruce-on-a-stick. An embarrassing epitaph for a tombstone.

Pulling on my parachute shrouds, I started swaying like a pendulum beneath my canopy as the post drew rapidly closer. I also pressed my legs together.

At the apex of my pendulum swing, I just missed the pole. I could swear it brushed my back. I crashed into a deep ditch just beyond it, which was considerately filled with smelly brackish water.

My girl, who had watched my descent through binoculars, later confirmed how close I'd come to getting a pole up my backside. That was two close calls in two jumps. She sweetly inquired how much longer would I tempt fate?

She needn't have worried. Half-way back to the hanger, I'd already decided that this sport wasn't for me. I'd stick to scuba diving. Swimming with sharks, moray eels, barracuda and string bikinis was much safer.

*(I still get nervous around fence posts and cows.)*

# Chapter Seven

## Off The Wall

# WHAT IF
# SUPERHEROES REALLY EXISTED?

*Spidey, it's about the goo...*

With the plethora of superhero movies Hollywood is producing these days, it got me thinking: what if superheroes existed in the real world? Imagine the mess Spider-Man would create with all those web-lines he leaves behind as he swings around the city every night. People would be outraged at seeing hundreds of yards of that sticky, ugly stuff hanging from tall buildings. And things would get caught in it: birds, hanging laundry, eloping teenagers. Oh sure, it's supposed to dissolve. Eventually. Meanwhile, citizens must put up with it. And how do we know that gooey substance isn't toxic? Spidey would be slapped with massive environmental fines. Littering, too.

What about the Flash, dashing around the city at super-speed? Consider the damage and distress from his sonic booms: shattered windows, crying babies, fallen cakes in ovens, mother-in-law tirades cut short. Who's going to pay for that? Plus the tribulation caused by his strong winds: toupees snatched off heads, papers scattered to all points of the compass, abrasive whirlwinds of street litter, skirts and kilts abruptly lifted skywards. He'd be arrested for being a public nuisance, at minimum.

Batman is almost as destructive as the villains he fights. His grappling hook would cause serious damage to building cornices and ornamental gargoyles. His indestructible Batmobile would mash cars as it roars through town, and rip chunks out of any building it hit. And the way he drives violates several dozen traffic laws. Does he even have a license plate on that thing?

Imagine Batman at a Motor Vehicle Bureau wicket, answering questions: "Address?"

"A cave."

"Accident and Liability Insurance?"

"Impossible to get for an unauthorized jet engine on wheels driven at high speeds in heavily populated areas."

"Valid Drive Clean sticker?"

"You gotta be kidding."

The bureaucrat would sniff: "License denied. And don't you glower at me, Mr. Dark Knight. As a civil servant, I'm immune." (Besides, the Batmobile looks like it only gets one kilometre to the litre, so the jet fuel costs would bankrupt billionaire Bruce Wayne.)

His compatriot, Superman, would have problems of his own: multiple class action lawsuits by women's groups across the country, concerned about exactly *how* he uses his x-ray vision....

Matt (Daredevil) Murdock would lose his law practice: "I'm awfully sorry, I couldn't prepare for your trial. I was out fighting crime all night."

Professor Xavier's School for Gifted Youngsters, used to teach his mutant X-Men, would slam into a more implacable foe than Magneto: our Ministry of Education, which would take a dim view of a curriculum that taught super-powered combat, advanced weapons handling, and covert missions that put underage youths in mortal danger. His school would be shut down faster than Wolverine can pop his claws.

Since most superheroes live in cities (to get better media coverage), that means supervillains always attack them there. (Evil megalomaniacs rarely request that heroes meet them outside of town to do battle.) Result: massive destruction of property, significant casualties and injuries. Insurance companies won't cover that. They'll add a "super-powered battles" exclusion clause to their policies, right under the "terrorist acts" exclusion they hastily created after 9/11. Even if government pays for the destruction, it still means taxpayers foot the bill. It would be cheaper and less traumatic just to let the supervillains take over the city. The never-ending headaches of running a city would be fitting punishment. Added benefit: short and disciplined council meetings, because the dictator/mayor's packing a death ray.

*(Look! Up in the sky! It's Writerman! No, no, waitaminute. It's just a fat bird.)*

# RETIRED SUPERHERO REUNION

*Time has not been kind to these caped crusaders*

Watching movies about superheroes, with their trim dynamic physiques, makes me wonder: What happens when these caped crusaders get old? Imagine a retired superhero reunion, where either the infirmities of age have finally caught up with them, or they have really let themselves go.

Let's listen in on two catty guests at that reunion:

"Oh look, there's Batman. My God, he's gotten fat!"

"Yeah, they say he can't fit into the Batmobile any more. And forget about swinging from rooftops - they can't make a Batline strong enough to hold him!"

"Here comes Spider-Man. Ugh, he makes Batman look anorexic! People shouldn't wear spandex if they look like the Michelin Man."

"I've heard he's so heavy, he can't stick to walls any more. And that Spider-sense of his, that warned him of danger? Now it only alerts him to when the all-you-can-eat buffets are closing."

"Speaking of buffets, do you see Wonder Woman over there? Talk about thunder thighs! And if she gets one more face lift, her belly button will be on her forehead."

"Never mind that. I wouldn't want to be standing next to her if that golden girdle gives way."

"Say, who's that confused-looking old guy there?"

"Oh, that's Green Lantern. Poor devil can't remember how to make his power ring work. The most powerful weapon in the universe, able to make real whatever its user imagines, on the finger of someone who forgets where he lives. So sad."

"What about that geezer hobbling along with a cane?"

"That's Superman. Can't fly anymore. Actually, most of his super-powers are kaput. He was exposed to Kryptonite once too often. But there's a rumour his x-ray vision still works just fine. I'm told he spends his days loitering outside high schools, staring at the girls' change rooms."

"That's disgusting! Why don't they arrest the old pervert?"

"Can't prove anything. Instead, they're reallocating money from the teachers' coffee budget to install lead-lined walls, which block x-rays."

"What's the big commotion at the entrance?"

"You remember the Incredible Hulk? When the army finally stopped chasing him years ago, he stopped getting exercise. He's now the Incredible Bulk. He can't even fit through a door!"

"Say, did you hear about Mr. Fantastic, of the Fantastic Four? All those years of stretching, now he's like an old rubber band that's lost its elasticity. These days, they keep him coiled in a box. And his wife, the Invisible Woman, now always stays invisible; she's so embarrassed at what age has done to her looks."

"How vain. What about the Human Torch?"

"Burned out at 50. Literally."

"The Thing?"

"Severe arthritis caused his rocky joints to seize. He's now a big orange statue in the park. Pigeons love him."

"Oh, there's the Flash in a wheelchair. What happened?"

"Remember how he always had to eat like a horse after he ran, because his super-speed metabolism made him so hungry? Well, he got adult onset diabetes several years ago, and wasn't careful one day. He passed out during a lengthy run, due to low blood sugar, and crashed into a building. Broke almost every bone in his body."

"Ouch."

"And Aquaman's crying over there, because he can't breathe underwater in the ocean anymore. He's on a strict low-sodium diet, due to hypertension, so salt water's taboo for him."

"Bummer. Hey, let's grab some punch, before Captain America drinks it all. He's so upset with his country's current government, he's become a real lush."

"Captain America? Wasn't he assassinated last year?"

*(I can still leap tall dessert carts in a single bound.)*

# THE CAPED STOCKING STUFFER

*Comic books have really changed since we were kids*

A friend and I were passing a local store advertising comic books, when she impulsively decided to pop in to buy some as Christmas stocking stuffers for her eight-year-old son. Because of a misspent youth reading comics, I appointed myself her expert advisor.

We soon discovered that, since we were kids, things had really changed in the colourful world of folks who wear their underwear on the outside.

First shock: the price. When she was a girl, comic books cost just 25 cents. (I remembered when they only cost 12 cents, but kept my mouth shut, refusing to date myself.) Today, most comics in Canada cost between $3.50 and $4.50. (Prices were even higher before our dollar got stronger.) Our government Scrooges do their part to encourage children to read by adding PST and GST. (How do kids afford comics nowadays? No wonder the neighbourhood junior capitalist cutting lawns and clearing snow now accepts credit cards.)

Second shock: which comics should she buy for her boy? A bewildering array of choices confounded us. There were comics obviously intended for younger kids, like Bugs Bunny and Mickey Mouse. But her son was now into superheroes.

We quickly realized there's no such thing as just a Spider-Man or Fantastic Four comic these days. All the popular capes 'n' tights characters star in four or five different monthly titles each.

Looking at Spider-Man's many comics, you'd swear he had multiple clones. There was one for beginning readers, several "regular-continuity" titles (each with completely-different storylines), one of a teenaged web-slinger that rewrote his history from when I was a lad, several mini-series, and one aimed at "mature readers" with extra helpings of violence.

However, Spidey is frugal compared to the X-Men; those merry mutants had enough separate titles to warrant their own specialty store.

Years ago, Superman and Batman, the icons who started it all, starred in two monthly comics each, plus some team-up titles. Today, it's four monthlies each, plus hordes of team-ups, mini-series and one-shot specials. (Makes you wonder why superheroes haven't formed a union to demand some down time. When do they eat or sleep, let alone wash their colourful spandex?)

One improvement: years ago, comics rarely featured capable female superheroes, who didn't always need rescuing by their male counterparts. Today, the ubiquitous Wonder Woman shares rack space (no pun intended, honest!) with many powerful lady crime-fighters. After careful investigation, I can report that some of them wear costumes that actually look functional, instead of skimpy outfits that any woman would fall out of while battling evildoers.

We also discovered comics for adults, filled with dark humour, cuss words, graphic violence, and sexual situations.

"Interesting!" said I.

"He's only eight," said she.

My friend wanted my advice. I said: "Maybe they have special Christmas-themed heroes, like Captain Candy Cane, The Masked Elf, Reindeer Pooper-Scooper Lad, or The Incredible Shrinking Radioactive Chimney-Slider?"

She gave me the same Look my wife gives me, on occasion. Desperate, I grabbed a couple of likely superhero titles and started flipping through them. The flipping got slower.

"Hey, the writing and art are really good! Much better than I remember." I started to read.

Exasperated, she solicited guidance from the friendly shopkeeper, who soon had her sorted out, while tartly informing me that: "this isn't a library, buddy!"

Ah, fond memories of my youth.

*(Each year, I ask Santa for the super-ability to clone myself. I get socks instead.)*

# GRAVEYARDS OF BAD IDEAS

*Where flops rest in peace*

Ben & Jerry's, the popular American ice cream company, have a graveyard behind their Vermont headquarters. There, 56 real tombstones, each topped with a winged cone ascending heavenward, mark the passing of a flavour that was a sales flop, such as Lemon Peppermint Carob Chip, Ricotta, Peanut Butter & Jelly, and Sweet Potato Pie.

What an interesting, if macabre, idea!

So, how about other graveyards commemorating bad ideas that didn't fly? For example:

**The Graveyard of Unpopular Vacation Destinations:** the Northern Ontario Outdoor Nudist Resort during sub-zero, black fly and mosquito seasons (eg: almost year-round). The B.C. Wilderness Forest Fire Trek. Afghanistan. The exciting Caribbean Hurricane Tour. The Guided Tour of Ontario's Heritage Outhouses. Chernobyl. The Spruce Bog Swamp Inn. The Octogenarians' Climb of Mount Everest. Lebanon. Toronto's mega-million-dollar Lord of the Rings musical. Moncton.

**The Graveyard of Giant Statues built to attract Tourists to Your Town:** The Giant Diaper ("It doesn't leak even after a heavy rain!"). World's Largest Athlete's Foot ("Stand upwind"). The Humongous Hagersville Tire Fire ("Bring marshmallows"). Canada's Biggest Mound of Ear Wax ("Contributions welcome"). The Behemoth Brassiere ("We have a *dream!*"). The Colossal Condom ("The *safest* town in Canada").

**The Graveyard of Unsuccessful Children's Games:** Pin the Tail on the Rhino. Live Snakes & Ladders. Monopoly, the Coroner's Edition. Explosive Squares Checkers. Battleship with Real Ammunition. Pass the Greased Pigs. Monopoly, the Sewer System Edition. Russian Roulette. Connect the Age Spots on

Grandma.  Hide & Seek Grandpa's Teeth.

**The Graveyard of Books that Flopped:** Home Surgery for Dummies.  How to Wrestle a Crocodile.  Raising Scorpions for Fun & Profit.  How to Catch a Bullet with your Teeth.  Do-It-Yourself Dentistry.  How to Win a Darwin Award (given to twits who successfully remove themselves from the gene pool through fatal accidents caused by their own stupidity).  Suicide for Dummies. Pimp your Kid's Tricycle.  Becoming an Ethical Politician. Cuddling your Adult Siberian Tiger.  Do-It-Yourself Bomb Defusing.  How to be an Honest Corporate CEO.  Bruce Gravel's Big Book of Humour.

**The Graveyard of Rejected Street Names:** Axe Murderer Avenue.  Flood Plain Lane.  Haunted Crescent.  Sewer Back-up Street.  Purple Poison Porpoise Pus Path.  City Dump Road. Overtaxed Boulevard.  Crime Alley.  Swampview Terrace. Dismemberment Drive.  Malodorous Mews.  Lovers' Leap Lane. Costco Circle.  The Completed Peterborough Parkway.

**The Graveyard of Failed Cars:** Edsel.  Bricklin.  DeLorean. Pinto.  Gremlin.  Lada.  The Tucker Torpedo.  The Amphibicar. Bulletproof convertibles.  Fuel-efficient Hummers.  Your first car.

**The Graveyard of Shunned Menu Items:** Tarantula Tourtiere.  Sasquatch Steaks.  Wombat Waffles.  Skunk Soup. Battered Bobcat Bouillabaisse.  Cockroach Crunch Cereal.  Sea Slug Stew.  Gopher Guts Gumbo.  Chocolate Covered Chipmunk. Bats 'n' Bites.  Truffles 'n' Spam.  Poison Ivy Salad.  Road Kill Surprise.  Last Week's Cafeteria Leftovers.  Wooly Mammoth Burgers.  Crunchy Frog.  Tooled Leather.

**The Graveyard of Misguided Inventions:** Lightweight Paper Mache Roof Shingles.  Battery-powered Baseball Bats. Doorless Bathrooms.  Silent Sirens.  The Most Comfortable Shoes in the World - only $4,500 a pair.  Hearses painted in day-glo psychedelic patterns, with matching coffins.  Mellow Classical Music for Teenagers.  Eight-Track Tapes.  Modest Bathing Suits.

**The Graveyard of Things We Used to Have:** Home delivery of milk and bread.  Our youth.  Inexpensive, reliable mail service. American tourists.  Banks that cared more about their customers than their shareholders.  More time.  A Canadian-owned Hudson's Bay Company.  The Beatles.  The magnificent Avro Arrow.  Fresh air. Enough family doctors. Courteous drivers. More freedom and less bureaucracy. Better weather. Drug-free respectable athletes. Inexpensive gasoline. Leisurely family dinners. Atari Pong. Cars with tail fins.

**The Best Graveyard of All:** The one without us in it.

*(I remain in grave condition.)*

# HOW TO SLOW DOWN TIME

*How bald men can become useful to society again*

Time.

For children, it seems to take forever ("Are we there yet?"). For teenagers, it IS forever ("I can't wait 'til I'm 16 so I can drive.").

Lucky kids. Time speeds up for adults ("It's my birthday AGAIN?"). Today, time zips by for us adults faster than vacationers stampeding for the buffet. Each year disappears quicker than the last. ("It's 2008? What happened to 2007? And I have no recollection of 2006 at all!")

Children grow up quicker. New TV shows get cancelled by the first commercial. More breakfasts are now eaten in the car, than at home. Week-long vacations are crammed into three-day getaways. Microwaves are used more often than ovens. People jump into relationships because they have no patience for long courtships.

You've just started to enjoy summer when, to the groans of your kids, Back-To-School displays pop up. Card stores unveil keepsake Christmas ornaments in July. The best selection of winter boots and skates is in August, the hottest month of the year.

Hallowe'en stuff starts materializing before Labour Day. Soon after, Christmas items start to appear, resulting in jolly Santas and cherubic angels arm-wrestling with macabre skeletons and baleful witches for shelf space. On November 1, with the ghouls barely snug in their crypts again, Christmas explodes mall-wide.

Seasons zoom by, with Easter arriving before you can pack Christmas into its boxes (you can spot those folks who have surrendered; their outdoor Christmas lights stay up year-round).

Back in the 1970s, futurists predicted that the dawn of the 21st century would see us blessed with more leisure time, like three-day weekends. Hah. Today, we're more time-starved than ever. Instead of the promised three-day weekend, we can barely hang onto the two days we have. (Because of the accuracy of their predictions, those 1970s futurists now work at Environment Canada.)

Why does time fly by faster each year? Well, the downfall of modern civilization did not start with the legalization of shopping.

It started with the invention of the clock.

So, to slow down time, we should ban clocks and go back to using sun dials.

Think of the benefits: overcast days would prevent us from telling time. So, new legislation would require that, on overcast days, we'd always get the day off. This would allow us to decompress and reconnect with what's important in our lives.

No more complaining about bad weather; we'd actually welcome it, since it grants us a statutory holiday. Don't worry about business productivity. How can our current productivity be sustained if we're so stressed out? Imagine how much more productive we'd be if, when we do work, we're re-energized and re-motivated! Why, we'd do twice the work in half the time.

Best of all: bald-headed men would become valuable to society again; on sunny days, their partners, friends and workmates would need them to tell time. How?

By tattooing a sun dial atop their chrome domes, then gluing on the upright thingie that casts the shadow (it's called a gnomon). Bonus: it would give us baldies a cool "time punk" look.

Men would no longer fret about losing their hair. They'd proudly display their portable time-piece.

Another benefit: people would be pried away from their computers (which, along with cell phones, would no longer be allowed to show the time) to visit the town square, location of each community's official large sun dial. Besides some healthful exercise, this would encourage face-to-face socializing again.

So for a better tomorrow, crush your clock today!

***(I can tell you the time off the top of my head.)***

# THE DOMESTIC OLYMPICS

## *Sports events around the house*

The Spirit of the Olympic Games rematerialises every two years, uniting the world, however briefly, in common pursuit of athletic excellence and product endorsements.

As our fine Canadian athletes strive to go higher, faster, stronger, it occurs to me that Olympic organizers have overlooked some major events.

If people are agitating to make ballroom dancing an Olympic sport, to say nothing of golf, frisbee tossing and hot dog gorging, then why not the unsung athletic endeavours that occur around the house?

I give you the Domestic Olympics:

**The 100-Yard Garbage Dash:** Happens once a week, when the half-awake householder realizes in shock that the garbage truck is lumbering down the street and the garbage has not even been gathered. Oh, the adrenaline rush as wastebaskets are hurriedly emptied while hurdling over obstacles (avoiding the deadly obstructions in teenagers' rooms get you extra points, as does even finding their wastebasket), kitchen waste gathered, and the garbage can dragged out to the curb just as the truck tries to pass you by.

And sometimes, you even think to put a robe on. Though the bunny slippers always look cute.

**The Get-The-Kids-Ready-For-School Pentathlon:** Happens Monday through Friday, in season, usually accompanied by unsportsmanlike cursing. This event has five components and doing them in order is highly recommended: Getting Them Up, Getting Them Fed, Getting Them Bathed, Getting Them Dressed, Getting Them The Heck Out The Door Before The Bus Comes.

For extra points: Chasing After Them With The Lunch They Forgot.

For an immediate Gold Medal: Getting You And Your Significant Other Out On Time Too.

**The Vacuuming Marathon:** Should happen weekly, but be honest, it's really monthly, right? Involves doing the house top to bottom with a howling beast that you always trip over (next time, put the dog out first). You get the Gold not for finishing the marathon, but for how clean the house actually is (points deducted for broken items, missed corners, and - coward - completely avoiding the teenager's room).

**The Newspaper Shot-Put:** Happens daily in many cities. Involves your paper boy/girl throwing your paper in the general direction of your front door. Gold medal if it lands at the door, six days out of seven. Silver medal if it comes to rest on the path leading to the door. Bronze if it hits the lawn.

Disqualified if it lands in a place where it won't be found until next Spring.

**The Shopping Bag Weightlift:** Happens weekly. Domestic athletes must carry as many cheap plastic bags crammed with heavy groceries from trunk to kitchen in one trip as they can, before the flimsy handles or bottoms tear.

**The High Dive:** What you do into your neighbour's pool from his roof. Bonus points if your bathing suit stays on.

**The Pole Vault:** Utilizing that pole your neighbour uses to clean the bottom of his pool to vault over the fence separating your backyards when said neighbour discovers you high diving into his pool without permission.

**The Hammock:** Self-explanatory. Gold Medal for successfully sleeping in it while the sweet summer air is filled with the soothing sounds of barking dogs, snarling lawn mowers, psychotic weedwackers, screaming kids and ringing phones.

**The Taxpayer:** This used to be an Olympic sport, involving hair-pulling, teeth-grinding, table-pounding and colourful epithets. Deemed too violent, it was replaced with boxing.

*(I'm training hard for when Mowing The Lawn becomes an Olympic sport.)*

# WACKY IN WACKIMAC

*Nutty naysayers numb a small city*

Smothered amidst miles of rolling farmland, deep in Eastern Ontario, lies the small city of Wackimac, population: 74,613 and one-half. How the sleepy burg received its unusual name is a matter of bored conjecture. One theory is Wackimac was derived from an old Gaelic word used by the area's early Scots settlers, meaning "grrrreat place for a still." Others say it came from the name of the settlers' leader, who was prone to irrational behaviour (usually involving equal parts whiskey and temper): Angus "Wacky" MacDonald.

Because of that still and its fertile soil, Wackimac took root and stumbled through history, slowly but stubbornly growing despite the best efforts of its ruling elite to keep it "small and manageable".

The city straddles the banks of the Woebegone River, a minor waterway that meanders in serpentine confusion through Eastern Ontario, and is so named because it insists on drying up into a mud flat each summer.

Wackimac, blessed with that wonderful "country air" whenever the surrounding fields get manured, is also blessed with a silent majority of hard-working citizens and dedicated volunteers, offset by a small but stridently-vocal minority who are dead-set against anything even hinting of change.

For example, when the town fathers (and mothers) wanted to honour the wishes of their elderly war veterans and erect a commemorative wall in the central square, a group of "concerned citizens" banded together to halt its construction.

They unearthed ancient documents that showed the central square had once been the traditional nesting place of the rare mullygully bird. The creature hadn't been seen in Wackimac in over 150 years, and was considered extinct by many ornithologists, but the naysayers insisted the veterans' memorial could not be built because it would destroy the mullygully bird's natural habitat.

The protesters, all 12 of them, were not swayed by arguments that the memorial would only occupy a small part of the square and, in fact, could provide a perch for a whole flock of mullygullies.

Letters were written, rallies were staged, and bureaucrats were browbeaten, with the result that, years later, the steadily-diminishing group of veterans still had no memorial wall and the ethereal mullygully was still MIA. (Although a tabloid newspaper did report a sighting at a gas station in Coboconk, along with Bigfoot and an attendant who looked an awful lot like Elvis.)

Another example was when Wackimac, usually forgotten by provincial legislators, received funding for a sorely-needed new hospital, a massive health centre that would serve the city and the surrounding region.

Of course, such a hospital needed a new direct access road, to facilitate the speedy passage of ambulances carrying wounded in desperate need of emergency care.

Of course, a small clutch of noisy naysayers promptly sprang into action, determined that there be no such road, because it simply made too much sense.

They stated the existing network of twisting narrow streets provided ample access, and cited a psychological study that claimed viewing the pleasant scenery of a tree-lined route through quaint neighbourhoods would calm the afflicted. When informed that ambulances were mostly windowless and prone patients on gurneys couldn't see out anyway, the authors of the study still insisted their conclusions were valid because, after all, they had PhDs.

To resolve the impasse, officials pried more money out of Queen's Park for a helicopter air ambulance service - which instantly upset those protesters blocking the veterans' wall, who claimed the choppers would surely do just that to the elusive mullygully bird should it ever reappear.

*(Any resemblance of Wackimac to Peterborough is purely coincidental.)*

# BATH BUTLER, PERSONAL THERAPIST, OR THONG?

*Hotel amenities we'd like to see*

A hundred years ago, a bar of soap in your hotel room meant you were staying in a fancy place. Some years later, shampoo and shower caps appeared. Then, since some travellers didn't realize face cloths were called that for a reason, shoe shine cloths were added.

In the last twenty years, there has been an explosion of hotel room amenities, to satisfy traveller expectations. Each hotel tries to outdo (or keep up with) the other.

As an hotel industry insider, I can testify that there is no end in sight for the proliferation of in-room amenities.

The international consulting firm of Grant Thornton LLP, conducted an extensive survey of current hotel amenities/services and discovered some outlandish offerings. Most innkeepers are shaking their heads at what some avant-garde hotels provide their guests. I kid you not, *these are all true:*

- 42 types of water offered by an in-house Water Sommelier (would that be someone who flunked the Wine Sommelier course?).
- Hot Chocolate and Tea Sommelier.
- Menu offering choice of pillows (fluffing service extra?).
- Personal oxygen dispenser.
- Designer "little black dress" with matching thong, in the closet for those unexpected special occasions (do men get a suave black suit with matching thong?).
- A Bath Butler to run your bath (does he/she stay to scrub your back?).
- A Tanning Butler, who comes complete with sunscreen holster (where do I apply for that job?).

It boggles the mind and makes one think: what's next?

Well, after several beers' thought and no consumer research whatsoever, I humbly offer these suggestions:

● An in-house therapist, to soothe your frazzled nerves after a long day of tense business meetings, or a long drive with squabbling kids.

● On-call computer geek to fix your laptop or Blackberry if it goes wonky.

● Personal Shopper to seek out unique "oh, how thoughtful of you" souvenirs for family and friends back home.

● In foreign countries, including Newfoundland, a Personal Guide/Translator/Chauffeur/Food Tester.

● A Shower Engineer to work those confusing modern single-dial taps so you don't get scalded or frozen.

● A Quiet-Time Enforcer, who'll silence loud talkers/parties/TVs in adjoining rooms, so you can get the good night's sleep you paid for. Authorized to use Extreme Force when necessary.

● A Personal Videographer to record your visit to the area, producing a lively travelogue that won't put your audience to sleep back home.

● A Drinking Buddy, who knows all the good local watering holes and laughs convincingly at your cherished time-worn jokes.

● A Card-playing or Golfing Buddy, whose skill level comes close to, but never exceeds, yours.

● Fully adjustable bed, that can raise the upper or lower body, with a powerful central spring that flings you out of bed when your clock alarm sounds.

● Plasma-screen TV in the bathroom, with 7.1 surroundsound speakers (7 wall-mounted speakers, and guess where the sub-woofer goes?)

● On-call Personal Trainer, who don't take no guff from nobody.

● Verbal abuser (or recipient) for those travellers who really miss their Significant Other.

● And best of all: a Personal Valet, who unpacks your clothes upon arrival, launders them during your stay, and packs them for departure, with the supernatural ability of also fitting all your souvenirs into your bulging suitcase and still closing it.

Despite causing an average room rate of $1,900 a night (and that's the seniors' rate), all these amenities would make your hotel room so inviting, that you'd never want to return home.

What a boost to tourism!

*(I think hotel rooms are better than home, because someone else cleans them.)*

# PARTY FAVOURS

*Political parties we'd sure enjoy*

All too often, it seems, federal elections are thrust upon us, giving us an intense sense of deja vu. Didn't we just go through this? Same issues, same parties? Ho-hum.

Since millions of our precious taxpayer dollars are spent on these retread elections, then at the very least, we should have a more exciting variety of political parties to entice our votes. So, as a public service, I humbly suggest these options (which already exist; they just need to be politicized):

**The Caribbean Beach Party:** their main policy platform would be the right of every fed-up-with-winter Canadian to go south for two weeks between December and April. To facilitate this, they'll buy the Turks & Caicos, making the islands our 11th province, with Canadian currency accepted at par. They'd win the election in a landslide.

**The Toga Party:** tapping into college nostalgia of baby boomers, all MPs of this party would wear togas in the House of Commons. Sobriety would be optional. In fact, inebriation may actually help the legislative process (it certainly didn't hurt Sir John A.).

**The Slumber Party:** elected on a platform of guaranteeing every Canadian a drug-free good night's sleep, accomplished by debating legislation endlessly. (Oh wait; established parties already do this.)

**The Tupperware Party:** their slogan would be: "Other parties promise a chicken in every pot. To handle the leftovers, we promise a set of Tupperware in every cupboard!"

**The Birthday Party:** free federally-funded birthday parties for all children, run by professional organizers (relieving parents of an ordeal clinically-proven to cause insanity). This party would also abolish all birthdays after the age of 50.

**The All-Night Party:** self-explanatory. Pets of their elected MPs would be called Party Animals; this would quickly become the nickname for the MPs themselves.

**The Bachelor/Bachelorette Party:** promising to get female and male strippers out of seedy bars and into private homes, a much nicer environment. Guaranteeing men and women nights of heavy drinking and wild abandon, with federally-funded fleets of taxis to haul plastered celebrants safely home.

**The Wedding Party:** a natural ally with the previous party should a minority government occur. Formalwear worn in Parliament by their elected MPs. Would abolish divorce lawyers and toasters as wedding gifts.

**The Tailgate Party:** offers tax breaks for purchases of pickup trucks manufactured in Canada. Also boosts our beef and brewing industries. Advocates drinking and NOT driving. Actually seeing, or remembering, the sporting event is optional.

**The Neighbourhood Block Party:** promotes frequent local social gatherings, because this environmentally-conscious party believes major expensive items should be shared among friendly neighbours, like snow blowers, lawn tractors, swimming pools, big screen TVs, sports cars, boats, wives, husbands.

**The Christmas Party:** proudly celebrating the Christian holiday with its traditions of frenzied shopping, debt accumulation and quarrelsome family gatherings. Their MPs wear Santa suits.

**The Hallowe'en Party:** why should people dress up in fun outlandish outfits only once a year? This party would legislate Hallowe'en costumes year-round. Imagine going to work dressed as your favorite superhero, monster, movie star, or homicidal maniac! Would put a whole new spin on customer service.

**The Dinner Party:** would provide tax breaks for restaurant dining, especially all-you-can-eat buffets, boosting our foodservice industry. Bonus: more business for weight-loss clinics, personal trainers and liposuction doctors.

**The Retirement Party:** fighting the misconception that all retirees are stubborn curmudgeons. Would make euchre an Olympic sport - or else.

**The Lingerie Party:** gets this event out of private houses and into the public House of Commons. TV ratings of CPAC, the Parliamentary channel, would soar. Their slogan: "Canadians are fed up with clandestine back-room deals. We'll expose Victoria's Secret!"

*(Personally, I support The Party Hearty.)*

# FACTORY SECONDS WE'D RATHER NOT SEE

### *Even if the price is right*

You sometimes hear about clothing stores having Factory Seconds sales at greatly-reduced prices, of items not up to the manufacturer's usual standards. If you don't mind minor imperfections like blouses missing several strategic buttons, or shirts with the cuffs sewn shut, such clothes are good deals.

It got our son thinking: are there Factory Seconds you don't *ever* want to see? There sure are. Proving that his college education wasn't wasted, he brainstormed most of the following examples:

**Seat belts.** Even if it saved a chunk of dough on the price of a new car, many folks would not trust their lives to sub-standard seat belts. Ditto air bags. Unless your mother-in-law always sits shotgun.

**Artillery shells.** Our hard-pressed military is chronically strapped for cash, but Factory Second shells are not the way to go. They'd likely not explode when they're supposed to, or detonate at the most inopportune times. Better to save money by having fewer high-ranking officers.

**Space Shuttles.** Brave astronauts, including my former Best Man, two-time Canadian astronaut Dr. Dave Williams (current holder of the Canadian spacewalk record), face enough challenges as it is, without the added risk of sub-standard shuttles that can't keep their foam together. NASA should find other ways to balance its budget, like selling tickets at $30 million a pop to space tourists. Why should the Russians get all that money? I know several people who'd love to launch their spouses into space. Using a shuttle would be a bonus.

**Condoms.** A definite non-seller, no matter how discounted the price. Playing Russian roulette is safer.

**Pacemakers.** Though it might be tempting at first, please don't buy dear old Granddad a Factory Second pacemaker. Even if it comes with a 30-day warranty.

**Life Jackets.** Though you'll probably only need them once, you don't want to cut corners with this item.

**Bulletproof Vests.** See above. Ditto for parachutes.

**Submarines.** It should be obvious that a country should never buy Factory Second subs. However, our federal government has never been accused of common sense. They bought four from the British Navy. (With four, we got Factory Second life jackets thrown in free.)

**Diapers.** Even though they are also only used once, trust me, you definitely want top-of-the-line on these articles. Diaper wardrobe malfunctions are far worse than saving a few bucks. Especially if the odious incident occurs when the little cherub is sitting on the knee of a beaming Grandma, who's wearing her best dress.

**Tires.** Factory Second tires are simply not a good risk. You need all the safety you can get, especially on those Ontario roads blessed with potholes capable of crippling army tanks.

**Steel-toed Work Boots.** You don't want to discover, after something crashes onto or cuts into your boot, that the steel toe has the thickness of a chewing gum wrapper. Factory Second hard hats are also not a good idea. (Except for hard-headed co-workers.)

**Airplanes.** Neither passengers nor crew would fly in sub-standard airplanes. It's just not worth risking your life to save money. Unfortunately, this mind-set doesn't extend to airline food.

**Propane Tanks.** It's not just about all that compressed gas under pressure in a sub-standard tank, or the high heat a propane barbeque generates. No, the real danger is having such a tank around those men who are already a hazard to life, limb and digestion every time they incinerate a meal. Call the EMS squad now!

*(I have a Factory Second brain with an expired warranty.)*

# THE WISE MAN'S WIFE

### Answers to 15 of life's Big Questions

You've heard the saying that behind every great man, stands a woman (who could have done it in half the time with one-quarter the complaining).

You've also heard tales about the Wise Old Man of the Mountain. So, in my neverending quest for truth, I recently climbed that Mountain and asked the following questions to the person who *really* knows all the answers: his wife.

**Q:** *"When I go boating, I often wreck my propeller on a rock. How come?"*

**A:** Your lake has mutant sentient rocks that leap up from the bottom to attack your propeller, because you've invaded their territory. Either that, or you're a lousy captain.

**Q:** *"Are Girl Guide cookies made from real Girl Guides?"*

**A:** No, they're made from Boy Scouts who've teased Girl Guides once too often. Lots of sugar is added to make the cookies edible, considering what boys are made from.

**Q:** *"Why is a female nude sculpture or painting considered art, but a female nude photo in a magazine is considered smut?"*

**A:** Because art galleries aren't allowed to buy smut with taxpayer dollars.

**Q:** *"Why is there air?"*

**A:** So I can hear your dumb questions. Also so you can order at drive-through speakers and cheer at sports events.

**Q:** *"Is it true that blondes have more fun?"*

**A:** No. Redheads, brunettes, black, grey, green and purple-haired have an equal amount of fun; it doesn't matter what colour a man's hair is. Unfortunately, this means bald men have no fun at all.

**Q:** *"I hear ya. Why do telemarketers and people doing*

*surveys always phone at dinnertime?"*

**A:** Because they're all on diets and feeling miserable, and figure if they can't eat, neither can you.

**Q:** *"Why do babies look so darn cute?"*

**A:** To compensate for changing their diapers.

**Q:** *"If space aliens exist, why haven't they landed openly, so we can all see them?"*

**A:** They don't want to disturb their funniest and longest-running TV reality show: The Amazing Human Race.

**Q:** *"If you kick the tires when checking out new cars at a dealership, what do you kick when checking out new boats?"*

**A:** The Captain.

**Q:** *"Many TV ads claim certain cat and dog foods are delicious. How do they know? Who tastes that stuff?"*

**A:** Starving would-be authors writing newspaper humour columns for free.

**Q:** *"If men are from Mars and women are from Venus, what planet are tax collectors from?"*

**A:** The planet whose name can't be said in polite company.

**Q:** *"What about dogs?"*

**A:** Pluto, of course. And it's still a damn planet, no matter what the scientists say.

**Q:** *"Whenever there is an election, lawn signs sprout up everywhere like dandelions. It's so confusing; who do I vote for?"*

**A:** Royal LePage, Century 21, Re/Max, and Messrs. Bowes & Cocks are always safe bets. Some even give you Air Miles for your vote.

**Q:** *"Why don't women barbeque?"*

**A:** Why don't men clean toilets? Wanna switch?

**Q:** *"Is it really true that man descended from the apes?"*

**A:** Definitely. Just look at typical male behavior, it's so obvious: the scratching, the laziness, the eagerness to fight. Woman, on the other hand, descended from God herself, and don't you ever forget it.

Now stop bothering me and go take out the garbage.

***(I'm still searching for the Meaning of Life.)***

# An Extra Helping of Dessert:

## An excerpt from
## Bruce Gravel's upcoming new humour novel,

## INN-SANITY: DIARY OF AN INNKEEPER VIRGIN

Think running a small motel is easy? Ellen and Pete Tomlinson sure did.

"How hard can it be?" scoffed Pete. "It's just a matter of making beds and cleaning bathrooms." Famous last words.

Ellen and Pete are a nice middle-aged couple who, fed up with their jobs and lives in the Big City, decide to chuck it all and start over. Believing it to be a "semi-retirement project", they buy a run-down motel on the outskirts of a small city in Eastern Ontario. They know nothing about being innkeepers.

Ellen pledges to keep a diary of their first year as motel operators and faithfully does so, as they embark on a wild roller-coaster ride unlike anything they imagined....

ଔ ଧ ଔ ଧ ଔ ଧ ଔ ଧ

Author Bruce Gravel has captained Canada's largest non-profit provincial association of innkeepers for the past 23 years. He has heard hundreds of true-life stories from many of the association's 1,000 members. He has incorporated many of these experiences into his first humour novel, *Inn-Sanity: Diary of an Innkeeper Virgin.* So 95% of what happens to these neophyte moteliers, are **actual incidents that have happened to real innkeepers.**

Hilarious things. Sad things. Outrageous things. Heartwarming things. What-the-heck-were-they-thinking? things. (And even spooky things.)

The novel will be published soon. To give you a taste, starting on the next page is **Chapter Two**, in its entirety. (If you're interested in the novel, email Bruce and he'll contact you when it's published, so you may purchase it at a special pre-order price. Email: bruce@brucegravel.ca)

# OUR SECOND WEEK

### In Which Pete Gets A Disagreeable Bath
### While I Check-in A Horse

Dear Diary:

*Monday:*

This week started bad and went downhill from there.

The morning mail contained a thick envelope from a law firm with more names than the starting line-up of the Toronto Blue Jays. Opening it, I started reading the letter. Two paragraphs in, I was hollering for Pete.

"We're being sued!" I exclaimed as he bounded into the office, out of breath.

Our place was called the Pleasant Holiday Inn. Charming name. Unfortunately, the worldwide Holiday Inn chain thought so too - and they had it trade-marked. Reading the multi-page letter, with frequent use of our dictionary to translate legalese into English, we pieced together the story.

Seems the previous owner, Hal Owens, had been receiving letters about this for over a year - first from Holiday Inn, then from their lawyers. Though the motel had been using that name since it opened in 1953, it had only recently come to Holiday Inn's attention. Owens had been warned to change the name, but he had ignored each increasingly-nasty letter. Now they were suing.

"Well, the solution's obvious," I said. "We can't fight Holiday Inn. We'll write and say we're the new owners and that we'll find a new name." Pete agreed and we sent off a letter.

And thus touched off The Great Name Debate.

## Tuesday:

For a couple that usually agreed on everything, we could not agree on a new name for our motel. We didn't want something obvious, like naming the place after the small city on whose outskirts we perched. The Wackimac Motel didn't float our boat. (Especially since we'd likely soon become known as the Wacky Motel.)

Nor was The Sparkling River Inn suitable, since the Woebegone River that flowed past our backyard only sparkled in spring. By early summer, it was stagnant. By late summer, it had expired into a mud flat.

In his ever-increasing dour moods, Pete suggested names like Dead End Motel or The Money Pit Inn. (In just one week, all by himself, he had managed to become wracked with doubts about our new career as innkeepers.)

I wanted something cozy and cheerful, like Mallard's Rest, in honour of the ducks that made their home along the river bank.

"But the ducks leave when the river dries up," The Pompous Idiot objected. "Hey, how about The Phantom River Inn, or The Departed Duck Depot?"

I threw a shoe at him.

We realized today that changing our name meant changing our road sign, our brochure and letterhead, and everything else with the old name on it. We had wanted a fresh look to our advertising materials, of course, but had planned to phase it in gradually. Now we had to do it all at once.

"Well, there's more money gone from our renovation fund," I said woefully.

That fund would take a major hit the next day. So would Pete.

## Wednesday:

We were doing chores, still arguing about names, when Angie, our housekeeper (otherwise known as The Human Dust Mop), approached us. Her expression was more gloomy than usual.

"Toilets won't flush," she muttered.

I looked at Pete, the de facto maintenance maestro of our little enterprise.

"Well, we gotta plunge 'em, I guess," he proclaimed.

He found a plunger, marched into a room, and attacked the toilet bowl with great zeal. It was the first toilet Pete had plunged in his life - at our Toronto condo, the custodian had handled all the maintenance.

*Sploog! Sploog! Sploog!* went the plunger. Great showers of water erupted from the bowl, landing in equal measure on the floor and Pete. But it still wouldn't flush when he tried it.

Dripping wet, Plumber Pete aggressively plunged the toilets in three other rooms, duplicating the mess in each. Same results: they still wouldn't flush.

Frustrated, he took a break while Angie and I swabbed up the water. After some thought, he said:

"Y'know, with the outside water line, when the well pump seized last week and after the new pump was installed, the plumber had to bleed the line to remove air bubbles, to get it to flow properly. Maybe it's the same principle with the sewer line. There's probably a big air bubble in it."

Pete used to teach high school. Not tech courses, but history. His expertise with hands-on repairs consisted of using his hands to search the Yellow Pages for help. Still, he seemed confident and his logic made sense in a Pete-sorta-way. I tagged along, in case he needed help. Or someone to call 911.

We went into the basement, where he found the plug at the end of our main sewer pipe. He took a big wrench to it with gusto. ("Gusto", to a male, means lots of sweating, straining and swearing - in equal proportions.)

The plug came off very suddenly and very fast, shooting past Pete like a cannon ball, barely missing him. I caught a quick glimpse of my man, eyes bulging in surprise, as a solid stream of foul brown waste water hit him and bowled him over.

Angie had silently materialized beside me.

"Huh," she said, watching as the rest of the pipe's reeking contents emptied onto my husband. "Shoulda kept his mouth shut."

Draped in that awful mess, coughing and spitting, Pete no

longer looked Pompous, but he sure had the Idiot part covered.

I could swear Angie was almost smiling.

The hastily-called plumber banished Pete from the basement while he fixed our system.  The plumber said that we should have shut off something called a sewage injector before taking that cap off.  Since our property slopes down away from the road, a sewage injector is needed to push the waste out to the main sewer line by the highway.  This means our main sewer pipe is under a lot of pressure.

Pete had found that out the hard way.

My hubby had to take several disinfectant showers, then get a shot at the hospital for what had landed in his mouth.

His motel name suggestions for the next few days were extremely colourful and have no place in this Diary.

### *Thursday:*

The day after the Sewer Incident,  Pete's father suddenly graced us with a visit.  Bowed with age, Bill moved slowly with the aid of a cane.  But his mind was still sharp, as was his mouth.  With large black-rimmed glasses dominating a thin severe face, he looked like a hawk moonlighting as a librarian.

He still had his driver's licence and loved to take rambling car trips all over North America.  It was his one remaining passion since his wife, after 46 years of marriage, had left the miserable old coot six months after he retired.  She simply could not put up with his grumpiness 24/7.  (No mortal woman could, unless she had severe masochistic tendencies.)  The divorce had deepened Bill's negative outlook of women in general and wives in particular.

He didn't much like me; despite my best efforts, we had never hit it off, even though I'd been married to his son for over two decades.  However, he was a major investor in our business: we had needed his money after the banks refused to loan us enough to buy the place on our own.

Thanks to someone's genius inspiration, Bill had been nick-named Sarge because of his stint as a Master Sargent in the U. S. Army during World War Two.  That background was still very evident as he toured the motel, passing out acerbic comments on what needed changing.

When Sarge found out that we had to rename the place and couldn't agree on a new name, he thought a minute, then suggested: "Why not call it Ellen's Fubar Motel?"

"Fubar? What's that mean?" I asked. "And what about Pete's name?"

Sarge fixed me with a shrewd look. "Fubar? Why, it doesn't mean anything, Ellen. Just like Xerox or Kodak, it's an invented name that will come to represent a unique product - in this case, your motel. And it should be just under your name, since a feminine name conjures a sense of home and comfort. Besides, I reckon buying this place was mostly your idea."

Pete sided with his dad (typical!). He liked the logic. My objections were overruled. So we called a local printer and started the ball rolling on new brochures and letterhead. She wasn't busy that time of year, so we had graphic designs ready for our approval early next morning.

Sarge left for home. He seemed amused by something. I mentioned it to Pete, but he shrugged it off.

*Friday:*

I got a phone call this morning from the local tourism bureau.

"Since you're not a member, we normally don't refer enquiries to you," the lady said tartly. "But there's a big horse show in town this weekend and every other place is full. Do you have any rooms available?"

I replied that I did. She hung up before I could thank her, or say that, as new owners, we were interested in joining the bureau.

One hour later, an expensive pickup truck pulling a gleaming white horse trailer arrived. "Crawford's Purebred Arabian Horses" was painted on the side of the trailer. Crawford himself was the driver. He rented our largest room, after first asking if it had air conditioning and if it worked. We were still in the middle of a major heat wave.

As I try to do with every guest, I chatted him up during the registration process and discovered he spoke about his horses the way most men talk about their wives or girlfriends. Then Crawford drove off, to spend the rest of the day and evening at the horse show.

Late that afternoon, Pete and I approved the artwork for our new brochures and told the printer to print 20,000 copies. I was a bit nervous with the large quantity, but Pete said: "we must distribute our brochure everywhere, over a wide area, El. Even though we're small, we have to think big! That's how we'll succeed."

I found myself getting used to our new name: Ellen's Fubar Motel. Had a nice ring to it. Maybe Sarge was finally declaring a cease-fire in our decades-long strained relationship.

### *Saturday:*

Early this morning, some very upset guests checked out of the rooms on either side of Number 17. They said there had been very weird noises all night in that room, which disturbed their sleep.

After they left, I realized that Number 17 was rented to the owner of that show horse, who had returned late last night. I went over to have a word. After some pounding on the door, it finally opened.

The smell hit me first.

"What have you been DOING in here?" I demanded of Crawford, who was standing bleary-eyed in the doorway wearing nothing but his boxers, blinking in the morning sunlight. "It smells like a BARN!"

The second thing to hit me was a big wet set of nostrils. Horse nostrils. Poking out past Crawford, from INSIDE the bedroom!

"My God! You brought your HORSE in with you!" I exclaimed, as I shoved the horse's head away from me. "Are you NUTS?"

"Not usually," he replied defensively. "It was far too hot and muggy to leave him outside in his trailer all night. And I was worried someone might steal him. This is, after all, a prize-winning Arabian! Don't worry, I brought in straw to cover the floor where he was, so there should be no damage to your carpet. I'll clean out the straw and his poop before I leave."

"Straw? POOP!" I was sputtering with rage. "I don't care if this nag won the Triple Crown! This is a MOTEL room, not a

STABLE! Have you no sense? You wouldn't try this at the Royal York Hotel in downtown Toronto, so why the blazes did you do it here?"

"Well," he replied archly, "this is not the fancy Royal York, is it? It's just a small country motel."

"Even here in the country, we know that bedrooms are for humans and barns are for animals!" I shot back. "Do you have ANY idea of how hard it's going to be to clean and disinfect this room? We take great pride in our rooms, Sir! They are NOT for the use of horses!"

Crawford fixed me with a crafty look: "Oh, really? Y'know lady, the Innkeeper's Act of Ontario states you must board the horses of your guests. That Act may be over 100 years old, but it's still valid."

The British have a unique expression for when something totally takes you by surprise, causing your jaw to drop and your eyes to look like saucers: gobsmacked. It perfectly describes how I looked and felt at that moment.

"Wh-what?" I said. "I've never heard of the Innkeeper's Act."

"Ignorance of the law is no excuse. Look it up: it says you gotta give me a room and you gotta board my horse, too."

"Well, it might very well say that, mister, but I'm damn sure it doesn't say we must let your horse stay in your room!"

"Since you don't have a barn, where the hell else could I put it? Say, you wouldn't know where I can buy more horse feed, do you? Used the last bag last night."

I just glared at him and pushed past him into the room. Which seemed much smaller with a full-grown horse in it. I quickly noticed that the bathroom door had been removed. Peering inside, I saw that the sink was now a container for oats. The bathtub was full of hay.

Normally I'm a cheerful person. But this morning I lost it.

When Pete found me, I had finished making venomous comments about Crawford's ancestors, and was working on the ancestors of his horse. The air was blue. Pete surveyed the scene and promptly took over the shouting. I left to see if we still had that shotgun among those unpacked boxes from our move here. If I found it, my next task was to call a dog food factory to find out the going rate for fresh purebred Arabian horse meat.

The horse and Crawford were gone before I returned. Lucky for them; I'd found the gun. Pete had charged the jerk a hefty amount to cover the cleaning bill.

Pete suggested we change our motel name again, to Inn Tolerable, or maybe Inn Frustration.

I wasn't very good company for the rest of that day.

### Sunday:

I had recovered most of my composure, following the trauma of the Horse Incident. After a mere two weeks as owners, Pete and I realized that for every bad-news customer, there were nine decent ones. (Which is what makes this business enjoyable, especially if you like people. It's also what keeps most innkeepers from committing suicide.)

I was checking out one of those nice people this morning: a charming elderly gentleman, touring Ontario with his wife. He noticed the artwork for our new brochure on the table behind our front desk, and laughed.

"What's so funny?" I asked as I gave him his credit card receipt.

"Why, that name on the brochure over there. I haven't heard that phrase since World War Two. It's a gag, isn't it?"

"Gag?" I said, as a small knot started in my stomach. "What do you mean? That's going to be the new name for this motel."

"It is? My dear, don't you realize what Fubar means?" When he saw that I did not, he went on: "Well I can't very well tell you because ... ah, it's language unsuitable for a lady's ears."

I was really concerned now. "Oh, don't worry about my ears. You should have been here yesterday - and Wednesday too, for that matter. So, what's Fubar mean?"

The old gentleman was silent for a long moment. Then he said:

"It came out of the Second World War. The Americans coined it, I believe, just like they did SNAFU. It's an acronym; FUBAR is short for F**ked Up Beyond All Recognition."

"Oh. Really. I. See." I said, and forced a smile.

I thanked the man for his information, and stood in the doorway waving until they had driven away. Then I tracked down my husband, while working myself into another monster rage.

"THAT'S what it means?" Pete was incredulous. Then he saw I was seething with fury.

"That miserable old father of yours set us up! He's an American war vet! He knew bloody well what Fubar meant! What a dirty trick to play on us! Especially on me: it's ELLEN'S Fubar Motel!"

I was yelling now. Pete stepped back before my verbal assault. Then his mouth fell open.

"Omigod!" he blurted "We've just ordered 20,000 brochures with that name!"

That shocked me into silence. Of course, being Sunday, we could not reach the printer to cancel the order.

"I'm sure she hasn't started printing it yet," I said, and almost believed it. "I'll call her first thing tomorrow."

"Unless something else happens," said Pete, thinking positively again.

Made in the USA
Middletown, DE
23 September 2022